Bc

PERSONAL FINANCES FOR MINISTERS

REVISED AND
UPDATED EDITION

by John C. Banker

w
THE WESTMINSTER PRESS
Philadelphia

Copyright © MCMLXVIII The Westminster Press

Revised and Updated Edition
Copyright © MCMLXXIII The Westminster Press

PUBLISHED BY THE WESTMINSTER PRESS ®
PHILADELPHIA, PENNSYLVANIA

PRINTED IN THE UNITED STATES OF AMERICA

Library of Congress Cataloging in Pubication Data

Banker, John C.
    Personal finances for ministers.

    1. Clergy—Finance, Personal. I. Title.
BV4397.B3   1973   332′ .024   73-5394
ISBN 0-664-24972-8

Contents

Foreword

Economists and the publishing industry have provided excellent books, large and small, on the management of family finances. This book on the management of family finances for ministers would be superfluous were it not for the many ways in which government, churches, and traditional practice make the money situation of a minister different from that of his fellow citizens.

As a minister, you are likely to live in a series of large houses and never own any house. You receive a regular payroll check, but the Social Security office considers you to be a self-employed person. You belong to a category of employment covered by Social Security, but, unlike all other citizens, religious principle could prevent your enrollment. If you live in a manse or parsonage, the use of that house is as good as income for you, but you pay no income tax on it. If you receive a housing allowance so that you may choose your own housing, you pay no income tax on the housing allowance (which makes you even with the minister who lives in a manse, but makes you quite uneven with Americans who are not ministers).

You entered your career with the knowledge that you would never become rich by so doing, and if by chance you are well-to-do, it would be unwise to be at all ostentatious about it. You began your financial life with certain assumptions about responsibility for others and for the program of your church, so that you are committed to being a giver to causes. You must decide how much to give and to what causes, but your neighbors have the further option about whether to give to anything at all.

This book is not for everybody, not even for every minister. It should be of greatest use to a seminary student who has begun his marriage and is beginning his career. (In one denomination, ministers have married at the age of twenty-three and have been ordained at the age of twenty-eight on the average.) The book will decrease in value for the man and the woman who is in the forties, because by that age, for good or for ill, patterns will be set and habits established. It will be of special value at age fifty-five (or after the last child is through college), when savings for retirement become possible and meaningful. It is but mildly recommended for ministers who are bachelors, for there is emphasis on typical family finance programs. The family with income substantially different from the $6,000 per year to $12,000 per year sample cash salaries and with fewer than or more than two children will have some simple calculations to make and will need to work somewhat harder to obtain equally constructive benefits.

This book is every bit as much for the minister's wife as for the minister. She has greater opportunity than he to control some areas of spending. She is expected, statistically, to live longer than he does, a circumstance that means that she may someday preside over family finances without him. Whenever the pronoun *you* occurs in the text, it may be assumed—unless the context declares otherwise—that the reference is plural: that *you* means the minister and his wife together, or even the minister and his wife and their children.

The author declares himself to be sympathetic about your family finances and the related problems. The topic is one in which the temptation is strong to be didactic, inflexible, and almost accusing. The attempt is not to make you uneasy, but to set you at ease. The aim is not to impose burdens of guilt and rituals of harsh bookkeeping, but to set you free from needless financial anxiety so that you may with abandon pursue your true calling in the gospel.

Chapter 1

FIRST THINGS FIRST

Any discussion of family finances is a discussion of priorities: that which you do first, that which you do next, and that which you do last. Priorities, however, are not always chronological. Sometimes you must do things of third importance or second importance at the same time as you do that which is of greatest importance.

As we turn these pages together, the notion of priority will be ever with us. What comes first? What ranks first?

The objects of our spending can range from the hard necessities to the frivolous. They are as numerous as an affluent and inventive society has been able to envision and construct. The causes for our giving are as numerous as the needs, the heartbreaks, and the joys of the human family. The devices for saving and expanding our money are as diverse as an imaginative system of human enterprise has been able to construct.

A few simple rules of priority should be listed, and everything else we say should flow from them:

1. Not as a matter of choice, but inevitably, the first use of money is to live on it. That includes the four obvious, rock-bottom elements of survival: food, shelter, clothing, and medical care.

2. A close and overlapping second in the use of money is provision for learning, for fun, for expanding the horizons of life beyond merely staying alive.

3. We will give to others as surely as we take care of ourselves and families, but the timing and the amount of giving are permitted to rank third in a mechanical list. Nevertheless, the happy giving of money cannot be deferred until all our own needs are met, lest it be deferred forever.

4. Saving is fourth, but it isn't fourth chronologically. Like giving, saving postponed is saving abandoned. We rank high, always in balance with other matters, the saving of at least enough money to provide for possible emergencies and major expenditures. A savings account of at least four months' salary is essential.

5. Along with a savings account there should be a sound scheme of life insurance equal to at least two or three years' salary to protect the family in the event of the death of the breadwinner.

6. Only after the above five items are well under way (they may never be completed, except at retirement time) should one invest in stocks and other securities. Before starting an investment program, one must be ready to live with market fluctuations and even adverse economic developments.

Every one of these topics is developed in the pages that follow. They are not fully developed, because nobody can do so short of preparing a graduate course which would involve infinite detail and study. It is important at this point only to remember that there are things that come first, either in sequence of accomplishment or in order of importance, or both.

Chapter 2

RESPONSIBILITY

Neither the nature of his calling nor the content of his training will equip a minister to be a skillful financier, but his Christian commitment requires him to be a responsible person. There is much, however, that invites him to be less than responsible. His congregation has promised to give the money for his salary, and presumably would continue his salary during some few months of illness. He is a member of a denominational pension plan. His fringe benefits may include medical and hospitalization insurance, and a major medical insurance plan as well. He is eligible for Social Security. College scholarships are largely based on need, and he is likely to feel that his salary is sufficiently low to qualify his children for aid. He may live in a state in which the government awards special educational assistance. Altogether, he is not to be blamed if he gets the impression that somehow he is going to be taken care of, and his family too.

Nevertheless, he and his wife are called upon to be responsible for a rational program of spending, giving, and saving. Without such a program, they often spend for things they do not really care about, they may give grudgingly and unwisely, and they will probably be borrowers rather than savers. If they are a couple who do not want to have a sense of responsibility about family finances, they may be in the wrong vocation, for a minister is committed to be a responsible person and this includes responsibility for "talents."

What is your present situation as a user of money? In the next chapter we will see ways of computing your true income and distributing it among the things you must do and the things you want to do. For the present, however, let us look at the roles you occupy financially.

Salary Contracts

We will assume that your income consists of a single modest salary or, in any case, a salary about which you do not complain that it is too high. In that sense, you have a contract with your congregation: you have agreed to be their pastor, with all that it connotes, and they have agreed to pay you the stipulated salary. In addition, however, you have another unwritten contract, and it is a contract with yourself: you have pledged to yourself that you will live at the level which the agreed salary permits. (If you receive salaries from two sources, consider the two salaries as representing the basic written contract.) You may say that prices are high, that the unforeseen is overwhelming, and that saving is impossible. Nevertheless, until something can be done about amending the first contract—with the congregation—the second contract stands and must be honored. You may never have thought of it, but your congregation assumed that you contracted with yourself to live at that level. Shortly, we shall speak of a plan that permits you to do so.

Negotiation of Salary

There is nothing sacred about the terms of the contract with the congregation. Not only *may* it be renegotiated; it *should be* renegotiated. A minister who is not up to such negotiations has a special problem as to leadership and human relations. He is likely to be one who has irrational uneasiness about accepting money for his work, and doubly irrational disquiet about negotiating for more. He secretly feels that not requesting negotiation or discussion is spiritually superior to raising the question. The problem comes into unpleasant focus when a special need or emergency arises. Made anxious by the special need, such ministers tend to be wrenched out of their usual attitude and to enter upon a kind of negotiation that is awkward and embarrassing to all concerned.

On the other hand, proper negotiation, at intervals (in contrast to frenzied negotiations), helps to establish not only the humanity of the minister but also the obligation of the church. Some denominations ask that pastoral salaries be reviewed at least once each year. Review does not mean necessarily an increase, but it means docketing for the appropriate meeting the matter of the pastor's compensation. It is senseless to have the review occur entirely outside his hearing. Only the minister can truly reveal how things are going and only he can furnish the facts on which the give-and-take between persons can make review meaningful. (Perhaps you should ask the church treasurer to comment on the financial advice given in this book!)

And the minister should be straightforward with his officers. There is something unlovely about the selfish, demanding minister, but there is also something unlovable about the minister who assumes a false posture of otherworldliness, self-sacrifice, and lack of concern for material things.

Stewardship

A by-product of negotiation about salary is that it opens up to the people of the church the larger question of their stewardship. It is not alone a self-serving process for the minister. There is an interesting parallel between the financial health of the minister and the financial health of the church. A recent study showed that ministers who are in financial difficulties usually preside over churches that are in financial difficulties. To be sure, many a case of that kind merely shows that the church was always poor and in debt and therefore underpays its pastor. In vast numbers of cases, however, the fiscal mess in the church reflects the fiscal mess in the minister's household. If the pastor is an improvident spendthrift, or if he is a man spiritually superior to the realities of money, he fails thereby to teach his people the financial responsibilities of a congregation.

We have seen that you are a contractor, both with yourself and your congregation, and that the terms of the contract are your compensation and your willingness to live within it. We have seen that you are a negotiator, in that you must assist in the regular review of your salary. You are a teacher of responsible Christian stewardship, because your care of money matters will be reflected in the care the congregation takes of its money. You have other roles as well.

Family Head

Surely you will be most conscious of your role as a family man. We begin with certain assumptions. You love one another. You care. You probably care especially about education. You will go even farther than that if the health, or life, of one of you is threatened. You will live without ostentation, but with dignity. Each of you will sometimes put the others in the family ahead of yourself. Each of you will sometimes want to put yourself ahead of the others.

But what else about your family, your particular family? It is either large or small, or in between. The precise number of members in the family—and we have not forgotten that your household may have some people other than husband, wife, and children— is an obvious statistic. It will inevitably govern many decisions about money. Three college educations, for example, usually cost three times as much as one.

It will be more difficult to say what *kind* of family you are, or, rather, what kind of family you aspire to be. What does your family desire from life, what are your real objectives? The differences between and among families in this area are significant and they are, moreover, legitimate. If all families were alike, it would be possible to publish nothing more than a table of budgets, with variations for the numbers of children, and demand that all follow the rule book.

Options

Happily, we vary from family to family. One family likes to travel. Another family likes to travel but prefers the short journey and the good motel to the long journey and the family tent. Still another family is more musical than anything else. Its spending for recordings will be out of line with that of other families, and it may decide that a baby grand piano is the way of fulfillment.

A wife may emphasize the physical condition of her house, so that her options for furniture would surprise the musically-minded. Her enthusiasm for household things may be derivative: her husband may be the one who wants a perfectly-kept household, furnished excellently, and she finds it good to show her affection by fulfilling his desires. Other families may like to set a good table, with or without guests, and that is their business, although we shall see later that the supermarket sales slip is one of the trickiest items to keep under control.

Enough. We could mention golf, theater, and reading matter if we were to continue to catalog the areas of optional spending that are really recreational. There are other options, however. Perhaps three children could go to large prestigious seats of learning, but the decision may be that all three go to smaller, church-related colleges, or to less expensive tax-supported state universities or community colleges, so that one of the three can also go on to graduate school. There will be another difference if one or more children should prepare for the ministry. Clearly, the kind of family you are, the aspirations you hold, the emphases you make, will govern some of your spending.

Giving

Another of your roles is that of Christian steward. Ministers vary in their giving, from the harassed soul who pledges something because it would not pay to have the church treasure know he gave nothing, all the way to the man who "tithes" his income before taxes or any other deductions. Of the making of books on Christian giving there is no end, and we shall here seek only a few generalized insights. A cardinal principle about tithing is that it should not separate Christians from one another, either on the ground that the tither feels superior or on the ground that the one who doesn't tithe imagines that the one who does tithe thinks he is superior.

Many factors in modern life have turned Christian people, including ministers and their families, away from tithing. They ask whether to give the church 10 percent of their income before taxes or after taxes. If before taxes, they may feel they are paying twice, because the people of the Old Testament apparently provided the cost of government from their tithes. Indeed, if a modern American were to count his share of the cost of government against his tithe, he would need to give nothing at all. If the decision is that a family will tithe, the question will remain as to whether the whole 10 percent must go to the church (and other giving must be additional giving) or whether the amount tithed shall be divided between the church and several charities.

"*Proportionate* giving" is the current phrase which suggests giving a set share of one's income, but not necessarily establishing 10 percent as the set share. Whether you tithe or give proportionately, it is important that you plan your giving in advance, preferably in the autumn of one year for the following calendar year, and that you give continuously. It is important also that man and wife be as nearly agreed as possible on the share to be given away. The children also may be consulted insofar as they are capable of consultation. There may be areas of family finance other than giving in which the children could be consulted as they grow older, but care should be taken to prevent consultation from being a phony exercise in which a ten-year-old is asked to help decide between a "compact" or a "normal" car.

When you decide among you what the share to be given will be, you should immediately say farewell to that sum of money. Never again, for the duration of that year, should you balance the giving of such money against the fulfillment of some desire of your own. Consider it given away before you cash your check. You will, of course, make a pledge to your church. That will presumably account for a major portion of your planned giving. Some should be set aside, however, for discretionary giving. It may even be wise to bank some of your intended giving over a long period of time, against the day when your congregation, or your denomination, may have a building fund campaign calling for extraordinary gifts over a brief interval.

Health Factors

Some years ago a religious magazine told the story of a family having numerous children who tithed an income of $3,600 a year, earned by the father as a trash collector. The article featured the detailed budget of the family. Most of the letters sent in by readers of the article pointed to serious and hurtful flaws in the budget. For example, there was no provision whatever for dental care for the children. Clearly, your decision about a share to be given away should not collide with the necessity for proper medical and dental care. The gift should be generous, and even sacrificial, but what should be sacrificed are those things you love selfishly, and not your responsibilities within the family.

When the amount has been decided, do as the great philanthropists do: regard the money as no longer your own. (They establish foundations and trusts.) You should establish simply a fund, regarding it as God's money, if you please. Then, like the philanthropists, give to causes of your choosing, from money which no longer belongs to you. Give wisely—you will find this very difficult to do! The ten-dollar gesture to a panhandler may be an act of irresponsibility when the needs of the wide world are considered.

Really to give wisely would mean learning everything there is to know about every cause that seeks help: especially the answers to questions about the administration of the money you give. If there is a mail-order campaign or heavy advertising in periodicals or on television, you must stop to wonder how much of your dollar goes to advertising and how much to pay salaries to the executives who gather in the money and then expend it. Better Business Bureaus have accurate records of such matters, and will tell you about the percentages (or will tell your businessman friend who is a member of the Bureau). Far be it from us to tell you to harden your heart. Just sharpen your mind.

Planning

We come now to planning your spending and keeping records of it, two topics so closely related that they are virtually one topic. Before we examine the records to be kept, let us ask who shall keep them. In general, it is recommended that the minister's wife keep the financial books. She has more day-to-day contact with the spending program, for it is she who goes to the supermarket and chooses clothing for the children. Moreover, the statistics say that she will probably outlive her husband, which means that she may someday have to look after the finances all by herself, and they will probably be reduced finances at that. If a man is unable to let his wife manage financial matters, he should probably take a look at his male ego. If he is one who "buys Jean a dryer," or says, "My refrigerator is ten years old," he is not up to the mutuality of planning and decision-making here called for. We recommend that he adjust his pride, and that his wife, perhaps at first protesting innocence of mathematics, make the effort to be on top of all financial topics. (It is equally wrong for the wife to handle all finances and the husband to be irresponsible and uninterested in money matters!) If the wife keeps the books, the minister should probably "balance the books" once a month to ensure a discussion of goals and objectives. In any case, all major financial decisions should be mutually discussed and agreed upon by husband and wife.

Planning your spending, giving, and saving is simply different terminology for the idea of budgeting. The trouble with the word *budget* is that it has irksome and inflexible connotations. It seems to say, "One fourth for food, one fourth for housing, no matter who you are or what you're like." *Planning* is a better word because it permits a program tailored to your needs and desires, and it keeps open the possibility of frequent adjustments as you journey through the program.

The kind of plan described in the next chapter is a yearly plan. That is the case because many items, such as heating costs and medical bills, cannot be dealt with on a weekly or even a monthly basis. They move upward or downward at different seasons of the year.

Data Collection

You begin by estimating how much you need to spend each month on basic necessities. The easiest ones to compute—not necessarily the easiest to pay—are the fixed charges such as payments on the car, for which there will be a monthly bill and a consistent due date. The easiest ones to forget are the annual expenses such as personal property taxes and life insurance premiums. They are big bills when they come, but they may not be on your mind at the time you make your annual plan. The hardest expenditures to guess ahead are food and clothing, two items where necessity and luxury overlap. If you haven't had a money plan until now, and have kept no records, you simply do not know how much you spend for table and apparel. You do know, or should, that some of your spending for food is optional and that much of it may be for the purchase of things you want, not need. Likewise, in the clothing store: you must wear clothing, of course, but a particular sport jacket at a particular price may be in the area of optional spending. Some items on your supermarket ticket may be toiletries, or drugs, or household detergents, or fertilizer and should be counted separately. If they are not, you will continually exceed your food budget, and perhaps not have enough to eat.

In these hard-to-estimate items, you will find the most help from the experience of others, as set forth in sample spending programs in this and other books. If you set out by following the lead of others, you will want to be particularly alert to the possibility of changing your plan as you go. The plan is of no use to you if it does not approximately describe the way you live. Hardest of all, of course, might be to change the way you live as you discover that your carefully thought out plan is in constant collision with what you do and want to do. If you are forever unable to save, and sometimes have to borrow, or unable to meet bills on time, you acutely need a spending plan, and may need to change your practices, if not indeed your tastes, as you discover where the leakage is.

Record-Keeping

Some people are always broke. Some other people with the same sort of household and the same income have saved and seem to meet unexpected costs with comparative ease—they made "savings a habit." The difference may conceivably be one of character and virtue, the one family being conscientious and prudent and the other being improvident. More likely, the difference between the families is that of having a plan and keeping records, or not.

Guided by the charts in the next chapter, write out your spending, giving, saving program. Plan to operate on a cash basis as soon as possible. We do not go so far as to reject all borrowing, as will be seen. Mortgages, though they do not apply to the majority of ministers, stand for more good than evil in the American economy. Few could afford to attain ownership of a house without mortgages. Without mortgages, fewer houses would be built. With fewer houses, more men would be without work, more people would be poorly housed. The same note may be made about major household appliances, though here we get more and more into the realm of items not strictly necessary. The important thing is to know what you are doing and what you are paying for the temporary use of somebody else's money. One of the biggest hidden leaks in family spending is the concealed amount that sometimes goes for finance charges. Later on we shall see how much it costs to borrow money in different ways. The spread in the charge for hiring money is wide indeed. You may do well to consolidate your existing debts in one place where the charges are least. It will have the further advantage of making you aware of the extent of your debts and of the urgency of paying off that item. The other goals you have will be more fun to attain when debt is no more and cash is the current basis for operating.

Capital Funds

An important step is to establish a family capital fund for future use, for emergencies, and for buying those items which would otherwise entail borrowing. We could simply call this process "saving," of course, but there is a little more to it than that. It means saving for more reasons than that thrift is a virtue. It means saving with a purpose, and thus making possible the attainment of the family goals you adopt at long range. It means earning interest on your capital fund at a modest rate instead of paying interest at an immoderate rate on your purchases.

The spending, giving, saving plan is complete when you establish the manner in which you will keep your records. A sample form for record-keeping is offered in the Appendix. It lists the costs of food, shelter (which you should show even if the congregation is providing a house for you), utilities, cleaning supplies, insurance, furnishings, repairs, clothing, medical care, transportation, expenses for vocational advancement, giving, personal care such as toiletries and barber and beauty shop, entertainment, vacation, pocket allowances, and savings. On the day when you really know what you are putting into each of these items of living, you are well down the road to successful management of your money.

Attitudes

These pages thus far have been an invitation to adopt a certain point of view about money and its use. They ask that you understand who you are and where you are financially, and that you make conscious decisions about where you are going. If you have bought this point of view, turn to the pages following and look for some precise and practical help.

Chapter 3

SPENDING PLANS

Your Real Income

Before we begin spending your money, let us see how much income you really have. For the purpose of this chapter, we will illustrate salary incomes of $6,000, $8,000, and $12,000 and make certain consistent assumptions. For example, we will assume that each minister and his family, at whichever salary level, will also have the free use of a manse or parsonage belonging to the congregation. For convenience, we will refer to the cash salaries—illustrated at $6,000, $8,000, and $12,000—in each case as the contract salary. It is the sum of money for which we have agreed to provide pastoral services, and it is the amount within which you have told yourself you will live.

Some note should be made of the amounts you may receive when you perform marriages or other services. Many ministers decline all such honoraria. Others accept them from persons not related to the life of the local church. In any case, if you count on them as income, you must list them when you estimate your income.

Every situation is special, and one special situation is that of the minister who has income from an inheritance. Another is that of the man who has noteworthy income from speaking engagements. If neither of these items figured in the initial discussions that led to the call to serve the congregation, then such income should be omitted from the present calculation of available income. They distort the contractual relationships, and they interfere with any future renegotiation of the pastoral contract. Perhaps they should be considered as sources of extra savings and special giving, and if so, the spending plan should be built before such additional income is taken into consideration.

The Manse or Parsonage

The manse itself is a special consideration. If you are given the free use of a manse, there would be something to be said for leaving it out of your estimate of income, and leaving any item for housing out of your spending plan. The difficulty would be that you could not then compare your spending plan with any typical published budgets, or make use of any guiding statistics set forth by the Government. For our purposes here, we will add to your income a cash value for the use of the manse, and we will show a similar cash value, when we come to housing, as an expense item. That will put you on a basis for possible comparison with your neighbors and fellow citizens.

If you can easily—and without starting a lot of talk—get an estimate from a real estate man as to the rental value of the manse, that is the figure to add in. If not, you should take 25 percent of the contract salary and use that estimate as the additional amount you are receiving by using the manse. Twenty-five percent is not a magic figure, but those who have examined the topic agree that it is a reasonably good current approximation.

We shall come to the matter again, when we look at taxes, but it should be noted here that a special tax situation applies to both manses and housing-allowances-in-lieu-of-manses. If you have the free use of a manse, you are not to report that fact to the Internal Revenue Service. The free use of the manse or parsonage is not subject to federal income tax. If you are accorded a cash allowance in lieu of a manse—*and if you really spend that sum for housing, as the Internal Revenue Service defines housing for clergymen*—you do not report that sum as income to the revenue people, since your housing allowance is not subject to federal income tax. We shall also see later a recommendation that if you receive a housing allowance and are serving a congregation, you use that allowance to rent a house or an apartment, for it is generally not wise for a minister serving a congregation to purchase real estate in the community in which he serves (but that is a matter for the chapter on investments).

Utilities

In any case, take your estimate of annual manse or parsonage value, or your housing allowance, and add it to your contract salary. Look at Chart A. There we observe the 25 percent procedure, and add $1,500 to the $6,000 salary, $2,000 to the $8,000 salary, and $3,000 to the $12,000 salary. In each case, we add the sum of $400, $500, and $600 respectively as *utilities*, which is just a guess at how much the congregation allows you in cash for utilities. (If the congregation pays all these bills instead of granting you an allowance, you should obtain from the treasurer the total paid for all these items for the past calendar year and use that figure.) It is not yet time to add up water, heat, light, telephone, garbage collection, and sewer rents. We come to them when we come to expenditures. This is the place for listing the housing allowance.

Adding manse and utilities to the $6,000 contract salary brings the figure to $7,900. For the $8,000 salary, the new figure is $10,500; for the $12,000 salary, it is $15,600.

These expanded figures may make more realistic any thought you give to the justice—so to speak—of the contract you have with your people. To be sure, the contemplation of the gross figure should not give any new sense of affluence. Rather, it should put in better perspective your income picture.

Deductions

Staying with Chart A, we begin to make the inevitable deductions in order to arrive at "income after taxes," or take-home pay, or money available for spending, giving, or saving.

Determine your probable federal income tax. As a minister, you are entitled to pay your taxes by making an estimate at the beginning of the year and paying one fourth at the close of each quarter. If you make such an annual estimate, you will know the approximate amount to list in your Chart A for income taxes. Many ministers arrange with their church treasurers to withhold their taxes, and the treasurer then remits them to the Internal Revenue Service at the required intervals. Even if you arrange for withholding and know what the total of the amounts to be withheld may be, the amount to list for federal income tax in Chart A is your actual annual tax (which may be more or less than the amount to be paid by the treasurer during the year or more or less than your estimate at the beginning of the year).

CHART A

A MINISTER'S*

CALCULATION OF SALARY FOR BUDGET PURPOSES

(His Annual Income Less Taxes)

Cash Salary**	$6,000	$8,000	$12,000
Manse or Parsonage Value ..	1,500	2,000	3,000
(25% of cash salary)			
Utilities (either an			
allowance or free use) ...	400	500	600
	$7,900	$10,500	$15,600

Federal Income Tax*	$450	$772	$1,512	
City Wage Tax or				
State Income Tax***	120	160	240	
	570	932	1,752	

Salary to Use for			
Budget Purposes	$7,330	$9,568	$13,848
	$611 per month	$798 per month	$1,154 per month

* For this estimate, it was assumed that there were four in the family (wife and two small children) and that the minister used the "standard deduction" for contributions, gifts, etc.

** A minister has many salaries—the salary he reports for federal income tax purposes (no parsonage reported), the salary he reports for Social Security (the parsonage is included), the salary on which his pension dues are paid, the salary used for state income taxes (if he lives in such a state), the salary which the congregation thinks he is paid, and the cash salary he actually receives. The salary calculated above for three sample situations shows how a minister should determine his "income less taxes" which will be used in his spending-saving program.

*** It was assumed that these would average about 2 percent of salary—but they vary widely between cities and states.

For Chart A, we have assumed a family of husband and wife plus two children, making four exemptions, and we have taken the *standard* deduction of 10 percent of income for such items as charitable contributions, taxes, and medical expense. (Most ministers should use Government Income Tax Form 1040, since it will normally result in paying less income tax.) Figure the tax as it really is for you and your family so that this amount may be taken from your gross income, and your *"income after taxes"* is properly ascertained. NOTE: Most budgets are based on "income after taxes" and not on a person's "contract salary."

Another item of taxation is any city or state wage or income tax that may apply to you depending on where you live. List the proper amount, after ascertaining the rate and the portion of your salary that is taxable. For the purposes of Chart A, we have assumed that everybody will owe such taxes to the extent of 2 percent of total income. There is considerable variation between cities and states, and in each category the salary bases on which taxes are collected is usually different from your income tax salary and from your Social Security salary! In the $6,000 column, we add $120. In the $8,000 column, we add $160, and in the $12,000 column, we add $240.

The deductions for taxes in the $6,000 sample total $570. When that amount is subtracted from gross income of $7,900, we have a remainder of $7,330. The taxes for the $8,000 column come to $932, and leave income of $9,568.

You are urged to do every calculation of your own income on the basis illustrated by Chart A. We are coming soon to certain imponderables and variables, and we cannot afford to address them with faulty income figures. So far as can be seen, there is nothing to prevent you from doing your Chart A right now (unless you have to wait until Monday to learn what certain tax rates really are).

Your Spending Plan

We come now to the heart of the matter—a list of the ways you will use your money: a budget, if you please, or a spending plan, or a spending-giving-saving plan. The caution must be reiterated: you cannot live on anybody else's plan. You must have your own. Nevertheless, we begin with a family of four, two of them being children under sixteen. Chart B tells the story for our three sample contract salaries of $6,000, $8,000, and $12,000, for which the effective salary for planning purposes (income counting manse value less taxes) is $7,330, $9,568, and $13,848, respectively. Indeed, when you divide by twelve, you discover that the available money per month in the three cases is $611, $798, and $1,154, respectively.

CHART B

SPENDING PLANS FOR FAMILY OF FOUR*

(These spending plans are not recommended for the minister. They are illustrative of how his parishioners spend their money.)

Items ***	($6,000 Salary) ** $611 a Month $	%	($8,000 Salary) ** $798 a Month $	%	($12,000 Salary) ** $1,154 a Month $	%
Food	$154	26%	$199	25%	$250	22%
Housing	72	12	104	13	169	15
Utilities	22	4	28	4	34	3
Furnishings & Equipment	25	4	30	4	56	5
Operations	30	4	29	4	46	4
Clothing	52	9	75	9	104	9
Medical Care	49	8	56	7	68	6
Personal Care	14	2	19	2	25	2
Gifts & Contributions	18	3	24	3	36	3
Reading	6	1	7	1	10	1
Recreation	17	3	23	3	39	3
Education	5	1	7	1	14	1
Transportation	75	12	96	12	138	12
Tobacco	6	1	9	1	12	1
Beverages	6	1	10	1	15	1
Personal Insurance	38	6	48	6	58	5
Savings	14	2	26	3	70	6
Miscellaneous	8	1	8	1	10	1
TOTALS	$611	100%	$798	100%	$1,154	100%

* These figures were compiled from samplings of families described as follows: (1) head of household, age 35 to 44; (2) two children, the eldest between 6 and 17 years of age; (3) a salaried —professional—executive head of household; (4) living in a city in the North Central Area of the U. S.; (5) only the head of household works.

** Note that ministers receiving these salaries plus manse and utilities have a monthly "income less taxes" of the amounts shown immediately below.

*** Most people who have not budgeted fail to be consistent about the classification of expenditures. As a help to those who need assistance initially, an explanation of these items is given on the page marked "Chart B Supplement." One may use one's own definitions within reason, but one must be consistent.

CHART B SUPPLEMENT

DEFINITION OF ITEMS

UNDER A NORMAL SPENDING PLAN

Food

Cost of food prepared at home and all meals out (including snacks) —at school, on vacations, at work, etc.

Housing

If home is rented, include total rent, whether utilities are included or not. If home is owned, include interest on mortgage, real estate taxes, property insurance, repairs and replacements. Include vacation homes and other lodging on trips, etc. If manse or parsonage is free, include its true value.

Utilities

Include fuel, light, water, garbage collections, sewage charges, water softening service, etc.

Furnishings and Equipment

Furniture, appliances, utensils, china, rugs, sheets, blankets, garden equipment, etc.

Operations

Include telephone, laundry and cleaning of items other than clothing, laundry supplies, domestic service including yardmen, baby-sitters, child care at day nurseries, repairs to furniture and equipment, postage and writing materials, garden supplies.

Clothing

Besides purchases of ready-made clothing, include yard goods, shoe repairs, and laundry and dry cleaning of clothing.

Medical Care

Health insurance (except loss-of-income), doctor, dental, and hospital bills, medicines, vitamins, eyeglasses, medical appliances and equipment.

Personal Care

Haircuts, waves, shampoos, soap, cosmetics, dental and shaving supplies.

Gifts and Contributions

Donations to churches and charities; all money given to persons not in family; Christmas, wedding, birthday gifts, etc., for persons outside the family.

Reading

Newspapers, magazines, and books other than school or technical books.

Recreation

Purchase and maintenance of television, radio, record player, musical instruments; sports equipment (except clothing and shoes); toys; club dues; hobby supplies; pets; admission to shows, concerts, and sports events. Do not include cost of food, lodging, and transportation on vacation trips, as these are covered under Food, Housing, Transportation, and Miscellaneous.

Education

Tuition and fees, books, supplies and equipment, music, dancing and other special lessons.

Transportation

Purchase and operation of automobile (including repairs, insurance, license plates, driver's license, gas, etc.) and public transportation.

Tobacco

Cigarettes, cigars, pipes, lighters, and other smokers' supplies.

Beverages

Coffee, cokes, beer, wine, and liquor consumed at home or in restaurants, etc.

Personal Insurance

Direct payments or deductions from pay for Social Security, retirement plans, life insurance premiums, premiums on insurance against loss of income because of disability. Do not include employer contributions to insurance or pension plan. Do not include health insurance premiums (other than loss-of-income); these are entered under Medical Care.

Savings

Add all increases in such assets as cash; savings accounts, including interest received and left on deposit; purchase of stock and any dividends reinvested; payments made toward the purchase of a home or other real estate. Also add any reduction of family debts (such as payments on the principal of a mortgage or repayment on a loan). Then subtract from the total any decrease in cash or savings; any sale of stocks, bonds, or real estate; any settlement under an insurance policy. Also subtract any new loans obtained by the family. If you end up with a minus figure, a "dis-saving," list it as a negative amount.

Miscellaneous

Interest on loans other than a mortgage loan; bank service charges; legal expenses; money lost or stolen; money allowances to children; all-expense tours and vacation trips where expenditures are lumped together; property insurance.

You must make up your own counterpart of Chart B, but notice some of the percentages and how they vary from one level of income to the other. For example, the amount for housing is higher when the income is higher, but the percentage is lower. One who has a higher income usually lives in better circumstances, but the percentage spent for housing usually is reduced (except for those with extremely high incomes). Food expenditures are larger in dollars when there is more income, but the amount spent for food is so small that the percentage often goes down as salaries increase. The reason is that the cost for food between two modest-income families just isn't very different. There is a limit to what one can spend for food (after steak, what else?) and an affluent person is unable to consume much more in quantity than a poor person.

Medical Expenses

Medical and dental care are items in which one might not expect a difference when incomes are different, because it is hardly to be expected that the lower-income family will have some cavities filled, and let others go, on the ground that they can afford only so many. Rather, the difference in dollars for dental and medical care is due to a difference in communities or a difference in neighborhoods or a difference in the doctors' charges. (Some doctors reduce their charges to ministers, though this practice is not as common as it used to be.) Care costs more in places where the income level is high, and the difference in dollars spent for it is generally more descriptive of where you live rather than of how much you care about good health. Here the percentage figure is controlling and stays the same at most middle levels of income. Medical costs are generally higher on the West Coast than in the Midwest or South and higher in Chicago, Cleveland, and New York than they are in Philadelphia or Baltimore.

Composite Spending Plan

Chart B is a guide only. Your own expenses are what count. Put down what you know your expenses to be. That is the way you have planned to spend your money. Your only duty to Chart B is to examine what it says in comparison to what you are doing, to see whether anything is considerably out of line. If it is, you must understand that it is, and you must understand why it is that your situation and the typical situation are so out of harmony. Some people like to pore over such a question, with pencil and paper and furrowed brow. Others arrange—and it is here recommended—a man-and-wife conference on the subject. The rewarding moment comes when both discover the reason for the discrepancies and discover further that they are sensible discrepancies—ones that will not seriously hamper the planning process.

Size of Family Differences

Of course, we cannot ask each minister to have a family of four, or if he does, to keep the children forever between six and sixteen. A major difference between your spending plan and Chart B will be the differences as to the number of children and the ages of the children. Chart C attempts to illuminate this difficult mathematical subject. It shows the extent to which the $6,000 contract salary ($611 per month for spending) needs to be reconsidered if there are few children or none, or if there are more than the typical number of children. We do not show here the $8,000 contract salary situation, because the matter is complex enough without it, and in any case it is the percentages that count. Chart C shows, for example, that a single person under thirty-five years would need only 35 percent as much money to live on as the sample family shown under the $6,000 column in Chart B. If the single person is between thirty-five and fifty-five years, he needs 36 percent as much as the sample family.

At the bottom of Chart C, notice that the family of six, with the oldest of the four children being over eighteen, will need 149 percent as much money as the sample family of four with two young children (i.e., 49 percent more). Appropriately enough, in the fifth line from the bottom of Chart C there is a family requiring exactly 100 percent of the amount needed by the sample family, and it proves to be a family of four with two children, the older child between six and fifteen years. That is why the line has a rule under it: it is the base line.

Obviously, if you have a $6,000 contract salary, and there are only two of you—husband and wife—and you are both under thirty-five, you will need only 49 percent of the money required for a family of four. That means there should be money "left over," and you must decide what to do with it. If you are enough under thirty-five that you are planning to have children, you will want to put some of the extra available money into savings. You will find more than enough uses for it later. There is a good case for increasing your contemplated giving when you are in the favorable situation near the top of Chart C. You will probably spend more for many of the items in your spending plan because the money is available: clothing, food, housing, for example. In any case, you will know that you are able to live at a level higher than the normal budget. The important thing is to know what you are doing, and why.

CHART C

RELATIVE COST OF LIVING

FOR FAMILIES OF DIFFERENT SIZES

(Basic Budget. See Chart B for family of four, with two children between 6 and 16)

	Relative Percent*
One- and Two-Person Families	
One person, under 35	35%
One person, 35-55	36
Husband, wife, under 35	49
Three-Person Families	
Husband, wife, under 35. One child under 6	62
Husband, wife, 35-55. One child, 6 to 16	82
One parent under 35. Two children	67
One parent, 35-55. Two children	76
Four- and Five-Person Families	
Husband, wife, under 35. Two children under 6	72
Husband, wife, 35-55. Two, the older child between 6 and 15	100
Husband, wife, 35-55. Two older children, 11 to 17	113
Husband, wife, 35-55. Three children, 6 to 15	116
Husband, wife, 35-55. Three children, oldest 16 or 17	128
Six Persons or More	
Husband, wife, four or more children, oldest over 18	149%

* These assume the same standard of living in the same general area as the standard family of four.

Indeed, you who have more income than you absolutely need may be in more danger of profligacy and debt than persons who have long had the desperate need to watch every penny. There are people with annual cash incomes of $15,000 who are more in debt now than they were when their income was smaller. The temptation is to live a little beyond available salary no matter what the salary is, and that little excess of spending often gets to be a big excess.

On the other hand, you may belong at the bottom of Chart C, where the number and the ages of the members of the family require almost a half more to provide a basic spending plan. Here, clearly, the situation is more difficult to resolve. You have only the dollars you had before you began to look at Chart C, and now you may be tempted to feel sorry for yourself.

Chart C, however, does not mean to tell you that you must immediately get your salary increased if you have three children in college! It means only that you need 49 percent more than somebody else (a family of four with two children, the older child between six and fifteen), whatever his salary and whatever yours, to maintain the same standard of daily living as that family of four. You must still live—and give—within your true salary, and Chart C shows that it will be harder for you than for some. There will still be people who have more children and less income than you, and they too have the problem set forth at the bottom of Chart C, but more so. The thing for you to do is to go back to your own private version of Chart B. If you have the Chart C problem that we have been talking about, you will find more useful than ever the typical percentages offered in Chart B—and you might give up smoking and drinking as a starter. (Chart C does make one think of "family planning," for it does cost more to support and educate a larger family.)

Salary Negotiations

We considered in an earlier chapter the matter of renegotiating your salary. If it is time for such a conference with your church officers, you might take Chart C with you if you have two or more older children. It shows, without your having to complain, that the increase, for example, in the number and ages of your children since the last salary negotiation may indicate the need for an increase in salary. If you have the facts (Chart B), such records help to show what your expenditures were for certain items as compared to the church allowances, such as for car expense, for entertaining the teen-agers, etc.

Clearly, any review of your salary must take into account the ability of the people to give and the degree of the church's success in leading them to give. It will also consider—perhaps silently—feelings about how well your work is going. No matter what the factors, church officers will surely be helped by a definitive answer to the implied question: How are things going financially for our pastor? Charts B and C set forth certain statistical facts of life in America today. If the officers know these facts, you are free from any necessity to speak grumblingly about the ages and the needs of your children.

Cost Leaks

Let us return to Chart B and its list of items in your money plan. We have already established that the figures in your Chart B must be your figures. Forgetting for the moment the figures, we should look at some of the items in the list to see whether there are places where you unknowingly get less than you should for your money. There may be hidden leaks that you can close without sacrifice.

One expert lists the following areas of unconscious overspending:

> High food bills
> Excessive finance charges
> High household operating cost (for fuel and utilities)
> High automobile expenses
> Recreation and children's activities
> Lack of knowledge of savings and investments
> Overpayment of income taxes

Some of the above items call for comment here. Others will be considered as we come to the chapters on banking and savings and on investments.

High Food Bills. This item, appropriately listed first, is the one on which a family not only may spend foolishly but may spend foolishly every day. We have already seen that it is important to separate from the supermarket ticket those items which are not food: cosmetics, drugs, lawn care supplies, cleaning agents. Having done so, we can then ask whether you are getting the most for your money. It is not proper in this book to tell you what to eat or how to cook it, but it is possible to list some questions that you should ask yourselves as you plan meals and shop for food.

Let's be brutally frank about it. You can buy an awful lot of oatmeal very cheaply, and with a little dried milk and a leaf of lettuce not only can you survive but you could probably be in better health than you are now. If you "eat to live," it doesn't have to cost much even today, but if you "live to eat," you can spend plenty. No one expects you to live on "oatmeal," but you should recognize that your expenditures for food generally are not based on "need" but on habit and desire!

Do you watch your meat spending? A useful rule says that meat is the largest item in your budget. It takes 24 percent of the average family's food budget. You probably cannot buy food wisely if you do not keep meat within the 24 percent limit.

Do you buy the right grade (of many items) for the right purpose? Eggs offer an example. Grade A eggs are required to have a thick white and a firm, high yolk. They are just right for poaching. In that manner of cooking, they look great. Grade B eggs have a thinner white and a flatter yolk. The yolk breaks easily. It is foolish to buy Grade A eggs and beat them into scrambled eggs. Grade B eggs are just as fresh and just as "good for you" and brown eggs are just as good as white eggs, etc., so you might save a little on an item like this.

Do you buy milk the least costly way? Surely you would not pay the extra cost of home delivery if you could avoid it. Milk and its derivative products rank second (after meat) in your food spending. In many areas, milk can now be bought in gallon containers at a lower cost than in quarts. Most milk will now last a week or two without going sour. Homogenized milk may cost more than whole milk and does little for you but to save you a brisk shake of the bottle. Powdered milk is cheaper and just as nourishing and not as fattening—but it doesn't taste as good, though some families mix fresh and powdered and find it satisfying.

Do you take full advantage of advertised supermarket specials? After a little experience with the same store, you can tell whether the specials represent the unloading of inferior items or the need to move along a large inventory of too many items of normal quality. If the latter, you should play along, buying the item that is especially listed on a particular weekend if it will meet the need you had in mind just as well as some other food you had been considering.

Do you watch the cost of ready-prepared foods? Not only grandmothers who yearn for the good old days in the kitchen but also trained home economists tell us to watch the cost of ready-to-eat foods. It cannot be denied that the new preparations are a boon to busy mothers—especially to busy mothers who are wives of ministers—but some foods are costly beyond their benefit. Canned soups are recommended for the thrifty because they save work out of all proportion to the added cost. Not so frozen soups, for they currently cost too much for the work they save. The semiprepared foods are the best economies. For instance, prepared cake mixes leave some work for the purchaser to do and still save time and work at little added cost.

Do you use the school lunch program? It is wasteful to pack a lunch for a youngster if there is a school lunch program. Apart from the social benefits of lunch with classmates, there is the fact that the Government pays fully 40 percent of the total cost of the lunch. Making the child's lunch from ingredients at home calls for no immediate out-of-pocket expenditure that morning, but the food comes from the store at your expense some time. Moreover, the school presumably has someone who looks out for balance in the school lunch diet.

The above are questions that may help you ask—and perhaps answer—more questions. If you want professional help, write to the editors of your favorite woman's magazine, and ask whether they have a booklet on economy in shopping and meal planning. Their magazine pages are meant to be very colorful—in part, because the food advertisers like it that way—and the result is that they show as many expensive dishes as they do economical ones. They will be glad to give you what they have in the way of economy meals. They will be glad you asked. (The U.S. Department of Agriculture issues excellent suggestions in booklets and pamphlets, too, costing ten cents to two dollars, and the Government will gladly send you a list of their publications. Address your letter of inquiry to: Superintendent of Documents, Government Printing Office, Washington, D.C. 20402.)

Some ministers' wives just don't know what a good healthful diet is and they are very sensitive if questioned. Most M.D.'s don't question their patients about their diets—partly because they have tried it and get such foolish answers. It will pay to get a good booklet on the latest recommended sample meals and healthful diets. The nutritionists have changed their recommendations based on new findings and the new menus are different from what they were twenty years ago. The Government has excellent and simple material on the subject. Every family should double-check on it at least every ten years. Too many families are eating what they like and taking vitamin pills to make up the deficiencies, but this is an expensive way which is not recommended.

Excessive Finance Charges. This subject will be treated in the chapter on saving. The thesis will be that it is better to earn money on savings than to spend money on interest on installment purchases.

High Household Operating Costs. High costs for fuel and utilities is an item difficult to control when you are living in a house that is not your own. The chances are that your church officers are aware of the size of the manse and have a general idea of the cost of heating (and perhaps cooling) it. What they will not usually know is that fuel may cost you quite a bit more than their estimate, all depending upon the *efficiency* of your heating system and the insulation of the house. If the biggest inefficiency is the leakage of heat at windows and doors, they may need caulking (which isn't expensive) or the house may need storm doors and windows. The question is who shall pay for them. If you do, you may leave for another parish before you save their cost in fuel bills. They seldom pay for themselves in less than five to seven years.

This is another topic for negotiation with your church officers. You will negotiate best if you really know what your fuel is costing. Meanwhile, you should have your heating system checked each year for safety as well as for efficiency: jets, nozzles, flues, and filters. Changing or cleaning filters can often save much at very little cost. A minister should see that these steps are taken even if the church pays the costs and is basically responsible for maintenance.

Nobody can help you save electricity in the ordinary course of every day, but a good habit is the turning off of lights, radio, and television in rooms where nobody is present. Children will tend to leave them lighted and playing, but you can save a penny here and there by turning them off. Don't be a grouch about it, however.

High Automobile Expense. You already know that there is a sense in which your automobile is more your master than your servant. If it stops working, you bring to bear all the necessary resources and energies to get it going again. When it requires unforeseen expenses to keep it going, you spend the money because the automobile is necessary. A few questions need to be asked. Perhaps you have already asked them of yourself.

Are you in the habit of buying bigger cars than you need? As one automobile finance man has said: "All that a car can give you is transportation. You're kidding yourself if you think you get anything else out of it, including status." If your car engine requires high-test gasoline, you are probably spending from thirty to forty dollars a year more than is necessary. A car that averages eighteen miles to a gallon versus thirteen miles to a gallon will save the average minister a hundred dollars a year in gas costs alone. In general, buying a good used car does result in savings, but the minister must have some mechanical sense or enlist the assistance of a knowing friend to obtain a bargain.

Are you spending too much for insurance? Of course you are. We all are. Nevertheless, there are some things we can do to help ourselves. It used to be possible to reduce your insurance costs by safe driving. Now it must be stated the other way: you will severely increase your insurance costs if you have accidents. Indeed, if you have more than one accident, the insurance company may cancel your insurance entirely. Some drivers are improperly keeping secret their accidents which run even into a few hundred dollars, lest they lose their right to be insured at standard rates for "public liability" insurance.

You might consider not having collision insurance on your own car, especially if it is an older car (over two years old) and has only a value which you could conceivably replace yourself. This leaves you with liability and property damage insurance to protect you against the claims of others. If you feel you must keep your collision insurance, elect as high a deductible as you can afford—$100 or more. Be sure to have enough liability insurance—at least $25,000 to $50,000 public liability—and much more is desirable. A $100,000 court suit against you can bankrupt you for life, and it may result from someone else driving your car!

Economy is not always to be equated with not spending. Spend what you must to keep your automobile and its tires in good and safe condition. It is false economy to cut corners on safety. Moreover, a car well kept will serve you longer and would enhance your trade-in prospects.

Above all, drive safely. In the age of the computer, your state's licensing bureau and the insurance companies jointly know everything about your record, and if you move to another state, the record often follows you.

Recreation and Children's Activities. Recreation expense is an item for ambivalence on the part of budget makers or budget advisers. On the one hand, nobody wants to be against recreation. On the other hand, it can be shown that recreation costs money—and probably more than you realize.

Who will not take his boys to a major-league baseball game? Who will not be glad for the occasion when all the family want, all at the same time, to go to the same motion picture? Bowling is popular these days, but some families enjoy it so much they have never realized that it has something to do with their general financial predicament. Golf and boating can cost dearly, but one can take care to keep expenses down.

Travel is costly too. Motels and motor inns are delightful, but they are expensive. Gasoline bought with a credit card never seems an extravagance. Even highway and bridge tolls add up.

The only advice we can give one another on money spent for recreation is the advice that runs through this book: know what you are doing. Keep records and make your future recreation decisions on the facts. There are recreational activities that are not expensive, so no one should be deprived of recreation.

Lack of Knowledge of Savings and Investments. For this item of money leakage, see the chapter on investments.

Overpayment of Income Taxes. The rule on federal income taxes is: Never *evade* taxes, for that is wrong and illegal; but always *avoid* taxes, for that is your legal and moral right and you should not pay taxes you do not owe. This is the advice given by the Internal Revenue Service.

Excellent income tax guides are available, usually at the book counter in the drugstore. For a dollar or two, they tell you what you may and may not do in completing your income tax form. The average minister needs a reminder of items that he may have forgotten, so he should review such booklets at least once every five years. In the large cities, an Internal Revenue agent will help you fill out your income tax form if you ask him at a time when the office is not too busy. Some ministers have found that it has paid them to have an expert fill out their income tax form—he will often save more than his charge—and the minister can then do it himself in subsequent years. This is especially true if a minister owns his own house and has had some investment transactions during the year.

Some denominations publish income tax guides for ministers. If you can get such a guide—a current one always—do so, for it usually contains sample forms that are completed and that are very suggestive. Such a guide may help you with your housing allowance. If you are one of the relatively few who are buying a house with a mortgage, you should know that the monthly payments often cover principal, interest, and taxes. If you are called upon to justify your use of the housing allowance for housing, you may use all three—principal, interest, and taxes—to prove that the housing allowance was fully used to house yourself and your family (and is therefore not to be counted as taxable income). *Then,* when you come to listing your deductions for medical care, contributions, interest, and taxes, you may *again* reduce your taxable income to the extent of the interest and taxes on your house.

The worst mistake you can make is to assume that income tax matters are really very simple and that you can go full steam ahead without any study or thought, or that you can do what someone else claimed he did (and got by with it). It takes care and attention if you are to save on some items. For example, we talked a few paragraphs back about not insuring your car against collision, or buying collision insurance with a large deductible. Did you know that the cost of a collision (maybe you hit a tree) which you paid for yourself, to the extent that it exceeds $100, could be deducted from your taxable income? Will you remember that when you fill out your final papers almost a year later? Have you kept a record of all your medical bills for the year? Read the tax guides, by all means.

Summary

This chapter has set forth some principles for your money plan. It provides you with starting figures, based on the experiences of others, and invites you to make your own figures, based on both the experiences of others and your knowledge of your own life patterns. It attempts to be practical, dealing with items as different from each other as the cost of eggs and bridge tolls. Nevertheless, it has only one message, often repeated: Know what you are doing. And the only way to know what you are doing is to keep a record of what you have done.

If you refuse to keep a record of your expenses and if you refuse to make your own private spending plan and reduce it to writing, then you might as well stop here and read a novel or a book on theology. That record is the backbone of all your financial planning. Without it, the rest is of secondary value. If your theory of spending is to spend as little as possible on everything—particularly any cash outlays—and therefore you assume that it is a waste of time to formulate a spending plan, think again. Thousands have tried that theory before you, and it just doesn't work. Furthermore, such a theory of spending is self-defeating, for it makes you feel frustrated and penurious, so you will not follow it for long. A spending plan can be creative and a real source of comfort not only to you but perhaps more importantly to your wife. We cannot recommend it too strongly!

If you do not know exactly how your expenditures are being made, keep a record—but keep it simple. Fill it in regularly once a day. You will not need to do this all your life, but you should do it at intervals just to keep yourself informed. Use any system you like—there are plenty of blank record books available. It should not be elaborate. You can line out your own sheet easily on two blank sheets of 8½″ x 11″ paper, and you are more likely to have pride in it if you do. A sample record sheet which you could copy is shown in the Appendix. It will last a month! Change the headings to suit your purposes or use it "as is." When will you start?

Chapter 4

DEBTS AND BORROWING

We are eager to get on to the next chapter, the one on saving. We cannot, however, approach it until we talk about debt. It is a loaded word: it conjures up a debtors prison in eighteenth-century England. It summons to mind frugal American forebears to whom debt was more a terror than was disease. It is the subject of many an aphorism. Even Polonius did not want Laertes "a borrower or a lender" to be.

Moreover, on pages like these, debt is the word likely to evoke homilies, and even to repel the reader with preaching. Let us try, however, to be realistic and fair. To be realistic, let us begin by saying that you probably have debts. Let us also say that, at least some of them are good, wise, and proper debts.

Debts would not exist if we did not have the practice of extending credit to one another. The Federal Government, and most lower levels of government, have big debts, because they have borrowed from the American people. The large corporations of America all borrow money, lots of it. Oddly enough, it may well be the nonprofit and charitable sectors of the economy which do the least borrowing and have the least debt. If wealthy groups and persons have debts, poorer persons who may need money even more are not acting irresponsibly when they assume some debts. In any case, debt is neither a good nor a bad word.

While it may not apply to you, as a minister and family, it is certainly true that most young families could not buy the houses they live in if mortgages were not available. Having a mortgage is not bad, but it can go too far: having a second mortgage is normally inadvisable. A second mortgage and a first mortgage, together, may add up to 95 percent or nearly 100 percent of the cost of the house. Some lenders will provide as much as 75 percent as a first mortgage. The remainder is expected as a down payment. People having no source of their own for the down payment then resort to a second mortgage to close the gap. Some are able to avoid the double arrangement by getting an FHA mortgage, which may cover 90 percent of the purchase price.

The second mortgage, however, is the thing to watch. It is called a "second" mortgage because the lender of that sum, if things go wrong, comes second in getting his money back after a fore-closure and forced sale. The owner of the first mortgage gets all of his money first and if there is any left over, the balance is given to the owner of the second mortgage. Because he is not so well protected in his investment, the holder of the second mortgage will want a higher interest rate. There are such things as third and fourth mortgages, but they are so exceptional and expensive that they need no explanation in this text.

The contrast between the first and the second mortgage illu-minates the whole topic of interest rates. Assuming that any two lenders are equally honest—and don't always assume it—the one whose investment is secured by something of yours should charge you less interest than the one who holds no security. Indeed, there are those cynics who say that you cannot get a loan at a really good rate of interest unless you can prove that you don't need the loan at all. For example, if you had ten thousand dollars in a savings account in a bank, the bank would gladly arrange to lend you five thousand dollars (provided you put five thousand of the ten thou-sand dollars up as collateral).

The fact is that you normally shouldn't borrow five thousand dollars if you have ten thousand dollars in the bank. You should withdraw the amount you need, because you can count on it that the bank isn't going to pay you more interest on your savings account than it will charge you on your loan. The bank is in busi-ness to make its own profit and it does that, in part, by lending the savings of its depositors at a greater interest rate than it pays for the privilege of holding the deposits.

All these observations lead to the truism that you can't talk about saving without talking about borrowing. If your family has debts, you ought not to begin to save until you have the debts paid off, because you are on a ground-losing treadmill if you do. The best use of money you have available for saving is to lend it to yourself, which is another way of saying: Use it to reduce your debt. The exception would be that a savings account for emergencies is always desirable. One should not wait twenty years for the retirement of a mortgage before putting something aside for a rainy day.

Over against the above paragraph is a psychological consideration. If you have a long-term indebtedness on which you are not permitted to pay any more rapidly than agreed, as is the case with some mortgages, you should begin to "save." Also if you have an old, low-interest mortgage, you might be able to earn more on your savings or investment program so it might be better not to pay it off. You should not use your indebtedness as an excuse for not saving.

The first recommendation is that you get out of debt and on a cash basis as soon as possible. It is impossible to talk meaningfully about saving until that is done.

The second recommendation is that if you must borrow, borrow as small a sum of money as you can get by with. If you are buying an automobile, try to buy it for cash, but if that is not possible, reduce the amount of the loan by paying as much cash as possible. Then, make your monthly payments as large as you can. Do not settle for the smallest monthly amount the lender will permit. Studying the question of the largest monthly payments will give you pause about borrowing at all. If you are already committed—in terms of expenditures and paying off loans— up to the full measure of your available monthly cash, where are these new payments to come from?

Don't borrow in advance of your need. That is to say, don't borrow for two purchases, several months apart, at the time of the first one. Borrow only the amount you need immediately. Borrowing these days, perhaps alas, can be accomplished in a very few hours.

Borrow from the least expensive source, not the handiest. The handiest source may be the people from whom you are buying. Indeed, they may be making more money as lenders than as merchants. Don't expect to delight the auto salesman if you tell him you will pay cash for the new car: he is a moneylender too.

It is important that you know the true rate you are paying for money. It may even be that you can find a better rate than you are paying and should consolidate several loans in the one new place where it costs less. Before you do, of course, be sure there isn't some large penalty for deserting the former sources.

The first thing to know about interest rates is to know the difference between the stated rate and the true interest rate. For example, you might borrow $1,200 and intend to pay back $100 per month. The rate might be stated as 6 percent. If so, you would pay, at the end of the first month $100 plus $6 interest (6 percent of $1,200 divided by twelve), or $106. Then you would still owe $1,100. At the end of the second month, you would pay $100 plus $5.50 (6 percent of $1,100 divided by twelve), and so on. The result would be your paying back the $1,200 in twelve equal installments, plus $39 in interest.

In another situation, you might borrow $1,200 at so-called installment rates. In this case, you would pay back in the course of the year $1,200 plus $72 interest (6 percent on the whole $1,200), even though you did not have the use of the whole $1,200 for the whole year. In general, you may estimate that installment rates are about twice as high as the "stated rate." The 6 percent quoted to you actually amounts to close to 12 percent, and you should know that you are paying it if you are. (In the above examples, you paid $72 for borrowing $1,200 in one case and only $39 for borrowing the same amount in the other or about twice as much. The "trick" is that you did not borrow $1,200 for one year, since you were reducing the loan each month—actually the "average" loan ($1,200 the first month, $1,100 the second, etc., and only $100 the last month) was only a little more than $600 during the year.

Chart D shows the comparative cost of loans from various sources. As you see, small loan companies charge the most. It follows our rule: They have the least security, since they lend after simply calling somebody to see whether you are employed where you say you are. Their rates in some states can go as high as 42 percent per year. Do not think of these loan companies as "cheats." They have to charge that amount to stay in business, because some of the borrowers "disappear" and never pay the debt. The other borrowers have to make up these losses.

CHART D

NORMAL INTEREST RATES CHARGED*

(On Loans to Individuals)

	Typical Rates	Approximate True Yearly Rate
Life Insurance Policies	5%–6%	5%–6%
Bank Personal Loans	$4–$7 per $100	8%–14%
Bank "Ready Credit" Loans	1%–1½% (month)	12%–18%
Small Loan Companies	1½%–3½% (month)	18%–42%
Retail Installment Credit ..	1%–2% (month)	12%–24%
Car Finance (Dealers)		
New Cars	$5–$7.50 per $100	10%–15%
Used Cars	$9–$18 per $100	18%–36%
Mortgages (Home)**	6%–8%	6%–8%
Second Mortgages**	9%–12%	9%–12%

* A new law requires the inclusion of a statement on the true annual rate of interest on most loan agreements. Read them carefully to make sure—including the fine print on credit card charges.

** Includes points, discounts, and bonuses.

Revolving charge accounts at department stores need to be watched. You apply only once, and thereafter you can charge almost anything you want, without applying again. The rates are high. The real damage is that you can become a borrower without going through any of the paraphernalia of borrowing. It is an invitation to borrow. When listing your obligations, remember department store and other credit accounts—anything on which you owe money—carpeting, furniture, gasoline, etc.

A credit card is both a splendid device and a deluding snare. It makes purchases, anywhere, almost anytime, quite simple. Unfortunately, the simplicity means painlessness, and that invites overspending. Having many credit cards complicates the situation, because it takes longer then for any one card issuer to get around to calling a halt. Own one if you must, but try not to use it except for emergencies.

If you have a credit card, be sure not to lose it. If you do lose it, report it promptly. A telegram or other message of record may be best, so as to establish the time and the fact of your report. Some companies offer credit card insurance, promising to pay for bills run up by the finder of your card or by the thief who took it.

Another rule is to watch out for resources you forget you have. One item might be the purchase of automobile tires or accessories. Four new tires might cost $100—enough so that you may be led to finance the purchase. If you have good credit with your gasoline company, they may let you pay one third of the price of such a purchase with each of your next three monthly bills at no interest whatever. However, if you could purchase four equivalent tires at another place for $80, it would pay to borrow the money from the bank.

Also, your life insurance policy probably has a cash or loan value that is available to you. If so, it is foolish to borrow elsewhere at high rates, since the insurance company will gladly lend the money to you at a very favorable rate. It is easy to borrow in this fashion. It is completely confidential. No questions are asked and no credit references are required. There is no maturity schedule, which means that you pay back at your convenience. Of course, the loan should be repaid as soon as possible to restore the full face value of your policy.

In general, other than from your life insurance company, your bank is the place to borrow. If there is a favorable interest rate available to you, it will be had from your bank. Parenthetically, there are credit unions that serve the employees of a particular industry or the members of a trade union, and their charges for lending money are usually very reasonable. There is no such credit union generally available to ministers, so we return again to your bank. (Do *not* borrow from relatives and especially *not* from parishioners—except as a last resort. Experience has proven this to be most unwise, so do not be tempted by friendly offers!)

Our rule still persists: The more security you have to offer, the more favorable the interest rate should be. If you have no security other than your hope of continued employment, you will pay the highest rate. At a bank, that rate will be something like 12 percent or more in terms of true interest rates, although the bank will describe it as 6 percent. If you have security in terms of the purchase you are making, you may obtain a lower rate. For example, if you are buying a brand-new automobile, the car itself provides some security (although the bank knows that it may be smashed in a collision, and so it will want it fully insured, and the bank knows that its secondhand value goes down about 30 percent a year).

The best security would be a bank account larger than the amount you want to borrow and in the same bank. We have seen that it would normally be foolish to borrow in that case. Lend yourself, so to speak, the money in your own account.

Stocks and bonds of known value are good security. If you "pledge" them, this means that the bank will hold them until you have paid off the loan, but the bank guarantees not to sell them unless you fail to pay off the loan at the time it is repayable. If you pledge enough security (more than the amount you are borrowing), the bank should give you the prime rate—a rate that banks give their best customers for the most secure loans. It is often 6 percent of the unpaid balance, which we call true bank interest.

When you apply for a loan, try to see the man in the bank with whom you have been dealing with respect to your savings and checking accounts. That is to say, if you went to the top when you first offered your deposit business, you should go there again when you borrow. Moreover, proceed with normal humility, but do not cringe in fear. While we want to preach against unnecessary borrowing in these pages, you should realize that lending money is the only way a bank makes money. If you buy a suit of clothes, you expect the merchant to thank you. That is how he earns his living. If you borrow, expect the banker to be glad you brought your business his way.

Changing the mood for a moment, however, you should go to the lender prepared to answer a number of questions. For example, if you have a loan elsewhere, he will need to know the outstanding balance and the rate at which you are paying it off. He will ask whether you have a savings account or a checking account or both and where you have them and how much is in them. He will inquire about your charge accounts and how much you owe. He will ask about your salary (and you'd be surprised how many ministers can't even answer that one!). He must ask your age, and that of your wife. He may need to know, depending on the kind of loan, how much life insurance you have. If there is a mortgage, you'll be asked about it too.

Therefore, go prepared. Psychology has its role here: if you seem businesslike and well organized, the loan comes easier. You need to know exactly what you want and how and when you expect to pay it off. In other words, don't say offhandedly that you want $1,000 when you really need only $890. In a large city bank, if you request $800, the banker may say, "Sure" and turn you over to the Personal Loan Department where you can get the $800 without collateral and possibly pay an effective interest rate of 12 percent to 24 percent, which are the "standard rates" charged on such loans. However, if you have collateral, explain that you want the money on a "promissory note" basis at minimum interest rates and that you wish to pay it off in one sum at the end of so many months and that you will provide adequate collateral. A promissory note is a legal paper that is just a "promise to pay"—usually a short form with less than one hundred words on it. Such an approach makes a good impression and you will get a much better deal. If you have collateral (stocks, an insurance policy with a cash value, some savings accounts, etc.), use it and do not accept the terms of a normal personal loan or small loan department. Of course, the collateral should be worth more than what you are borrowing—perhaps 25 percent more if it is common stock. You should realize that some forms of assets are useless as collateral for small short-term loans, such as household furniture, your car, your clothes, the value of your house in excess of the mortgage, etc. The reason for this is that it costs more to draw up the legal instruments that would give the bank a right to the property in case of default than the bank would earn in interest. Do not offer such assets, for no banker will accept them. His associates or the state bank examiner could make his life miserable if he tried it.

Special Advice

1. In dealing with a bank especially (though this is true of all business deals), you should act responsibly and precisely. If you are to pay $46.34 on the first of each month for twelve months, do so. Do not try to pay $50 one month, or an extra $10 on

the seventeenth, but stick by the terms of the agreement exactly until it is finished. Do not casually pay the amount on the third of the month if the first and second are Saturday and Sunday, when the bank is closed. Pay it the Friday before. Fulfilling the terms of your agreement precisely and not changing it will establish a good credit rating. Failure to do so will hurt your image.

2. It is not possible to establish a good "credit rating" in a community if you have been negligent about debt repayments. You need not worry about establishing a credit rating in advance —it isn't necessary. Your credit rating will follow you from one city to the next, so leaving one community with unpaid debts and moving to a new one in a different state doesn't clear your record. Your credit rating will be good if you have paid all charges promptly. This means department store bills, drugstore bills, credit card bills, etc., as well as notes to banks or other financial institutions. If you cannot pay as promised and go to an organization before a payment is overdue and explain the situation and set up a new way to meet the obligation, it will not adversely affect your credit rating. If, however, you are embarrassed and fail to take the initiative in talking it over before the due date, then you do get a black mark against your record and it takes a long time to reestablish your name as a financially responsible person.

If you are so much in debt that it all seems unreal, you may be in need of one of the many forms of financial counseling. As a clergyman, you should know what these agencies are. In a large city, you might go to "Family Service" in the social welfare department, or go to your bank. Often small loan companies (such as Household Finance) render valuable assistance. Perhaps a clergyman of another denomination will help you, but do get good advice and stay with it (until you can see daylight!). Collecting the information can be time-consuming and frustrating, but it is well worth it. Basically, you must know *all* the sources to which you owe money, their addresses and how much you owe them: doctors, dentists, department stores, service stations, drugstores, loan companies, school debts, tuition obligations, etc. In some cases, you will know precisely what you owe. In others, you may really have no idea, and in these cases, write (don't phone) and ask what it would cost to pay off all of your debt on *a certain* date (about two months ahead—say, March 30). Only when you have *all the facts* can someone help you intelligently, and if you don't write, your adviser will need to do it for you. You may need the explicit help of someone who will go over the whole picture with you. Do not hesitate to ask for such help, just as you have told many other people not to hesitate to ask for help when they need it.

We turn now from borrowing to saving. Saving is the converse of borrowing. Both are ways of doing, at a given point in time, that which could not be done from that month's paycheck. Both are good, but saving is better. If you have found these paragraphs on borrowing difficult to read—or to take—it may mean that your borrowing has gone out of control.

Now, let's talk about saving.

Chapter 5

SAVING

Saving is the process of setting aside some of today's income for future expenditure. It has the advantage that most money saved can be so placed that it will earn extra income while it awaits your call. As we have said, it is the exact opposite of borrowing.

There are many reasons for saving. It has a high place in the literature of virtue. "A penny saved is a penny earned," according to Poor Richard. Men of mighty wealth, such as Andrew Carnegie, saved their money, even their pennies. Our purpose here is not to make a mystic virtue of saving, but only to honor it for what it can do as a practical servant for you.

A minimal saving program would be one that serves to "even out" the demands for money during any one year. For example, a person might save money in the summer toward the winter fuel bill, so that the amount taken out of each paycheck for fuel would be the same, year around. Similarly, life insurance premiums and automobile and fire insurance premiums may be payable annually, and they would be difficult to meet on any one payday if you hadn't looked ahead. If you are paying your income tax in quarterly installments, you may find each installment too big to deal with when it arises, so you must prepare for it. One financial adviser tells families to take out separate bank accounts for each such major item. That is perhaps unrealistic. One family keeps it all in one checkbook, but keeps two tallies of the balance. The one tally, on the check stubs, shows only the balance that is available for immediate spending. At the back of the checkbook is a page on which certain portions of each deposit have been entered and which represent income tax payments, insurance, and other big amounts that are to come due. Adding the two balances together should come to the same balance as the bank shows each month, but keeping the two tallies prevents dipping into the long-range money for day-to-day needs—or seeming needs.

If you cannot do as suggested in the above paragraph—or cannot do the same thing in a better way—you are not ready for any longer-term plan of saving. If you are ready, we may then talk about a *capital* fund for the family.

Let us digress a moment to talk about *operating funds, endowment funds,* and *capital funds,* as they respectively affect the church in which you serve. If we can get them straight in our minds as to church denominations, it may help us get them straight for our purposes here—particularly as to capital funds. You know what operating funds are for your church. The treasurer pays your salary from that fund as well as the heating bill, repairs to the roof, music costs, etc. You know perhaps what endowment funds are. They usually arise from major gifts, more often than not in the form of bequests or wills, such as a bequest of $5,000 or a gift of one hundred shares of American Telephone & Telegraph (A.T.&T.) stock. The income derived from such funds is available for the use of the church, but not any part of the original gift, and only the income from the investment of those funds becomes a part of the operating fund. To be sure, the donor may have restricted the money as to which area of operations it is to be used in, such as for music, but the income still becomes part of the operating fund.

That leaves capital funds. Such money is needed to rehabilitate, or refurbish, or replace such solid structures as buildings for the new demands of each new age. By and large, denominations do not—or have not been able to—set aside money in advance for capital funds. The result is that they have, from generation to generation, building fund drives or capital fund drives to get the money to build or replace structures.

If you live in a manse, your two principal items of capital would be your household furnishings and your automobile. Both wear out. Both need maintenance even before they wear out. Both will need one day to be replaced. The purpose of a capital fund is to provide in advance, unlike the pattern in the denominations, for the day of replacement. Household furnishings are of two kinds these days: furniture and mechanical appliances. The furniture is the more manageable item, since an unsightly chair can be put where it is more or less unseen. A refrigerator that breaks down must be repaired or replaced, almost immediately. We have already seen that an automobile is like the refrigerator in that respect, perhaps even more so. The average working life-time of certain items used in a normal family is: refrigerator, 13 years; clothes washer, 6 to 8 years; clothes dryer, 10 to 12 years; automobile, 5 years; television, 5 years; radios, 10 years; etc.

Therefore you are urged to make your second level of saving the establishment of a family capital fund. The first level was to have enough money to pay annual costs when they become due—taxes, insurance, etc. Ideally, you would make a list of those items you own which will someday need to be replaced. You would add to it the items you will need or want: a dishwasher, three bicycles for three children at predetermined dates, etc. You should establish a program for retiring your larger pieces of furniture and replacing them with new items. A sofa that wears through in the most visible places will be no respecter of your furniture retirement schedule, nor will a bed whose innerspring mattress snaps a spring!

Nevertheless, you can dream aloud a little about the items for replacement or for addition to your household equipment. You can even be fairly precise about your scheduled automobile replacement needs. Make a list, a defective list to be sure, and see how much you need to save each month to keep ahead of the game. If you don't save the money from the paychecks that come before the needed purchase, you will take the money from the paychecks that come thereafter, and you will pay more for each item because you will be paying interest to the people who advance you the money.

Another level of saving—and who is to say that it comes before or after a capital fund in importance?—is saving ahead for emergencies. In the first pages of this book we talked about the temptation to forget about emergencies, because the minister may be led to believe that somehow he will always be "taken care of." We sought to dismiss that point of view on the ground of Christian responsibility. Nevertheless, here it is: the problem of the unforeseen and the degree of our responsibility to cope with it in advance. We do some of our duty when we buy insurance, but many emergencies are not insurable or it is not practical to insure against them (such as the breaking of a dental plate, or the death of a parent which requires a long unexpected trip).

No one can foresee emergencies. Indeed that is one of the definitions of an emergency: You don't know it's going to emerge. In today's society, emotional illness is a large factor in major illness. It is a kind of illness in which there is solid hope of a solid cure, but the surest cure in many cases is a long stay in an excellent hospital. America's best-known psychiatric hospital charges $90 per day. That comes to $2,800 per month, or $33,600 for a typical hospitalization. Even if a major medical plan were to pay, let us say, $25,000 of that sum, there would remain $8,600 for the patient and his family to pay. Now, it is possible for a congregation to pick up the $8,600 burden, but let us be realistic. If the pastor becomes ill enough to need hospitalization for emotional reasons, there is a good chance that the very illness itself has damaged his relations with his congregation, and they may not lovingly react to his need.

All these considerations—and others—suggest that the minister and his family save for emergencies as well as for future capital purchases and for the payment of possible medical bills of large size.

The other area of saving is that which we do for the long haul, just because it is a long haul, and we know that one day it will be too late to start saving. In that category, we place provision for the college education of children and provision for retirement. Retirement needs are hard to measure. For one thing, you may not live to retire. Perhaps neither you nor your wife will reach that age. If you do retire, it is anybody's guess how long you will live, either one of you. Meanwhile, you have, we assume, a pension plan. You have, or should have, been enrolled in Social Security. (We digress here to say that ministers are the only group in America who have a personal choice about participating in Social Security. It is a pity that it is so, because all should be in it.)

College is easier to calculate as to savings needs. Most families are saying that the cost of college away from home is at least $2,000 per year now and that it will be $3,000 per year in another ten years. To be sure, there are scholarships, loans, and other kinds of aid, and perhaps students should work for their education. Get a catalog from a good college at the other end of your state (so you can get some idea about transportation), and figure the costs versus the probable forms of aid and scholarship assistance. Figure how much a child might earn, both summers and during the academic terms. Get a general idea how much is left for you to do. Thus you have an idea how much you must save between today and the spring of the senior year of the youngest of the children. It may be necessary for your wife to go back to work to earn enough extra money to meet some of these needs, and if that is the only way it can be done, some special planning may be advisable. In some instances it may be possible for the child to stay at home while attending college (some ministers move in order to make this possible), and this can effect large savings. In still other situations the children plan to stay out of school a while to earn enough to attend comfortably a college of their choice while others find a "cooperative" program combining work and education. There are innumerable ways to accomplish the objective, so do not be overly discouraged. It is a point at which family planning is of particular importance.

Seeing all that there is to be saved for, you will agree that it would be good for your children to learn now about saving. If you had experiences with saving as a child, you may find less need than most for this chapter. If you didn't get acquainted with savings and banks and interest, you may wish you had. As we come next to the matter of banking, we will examine the kinds of accounts there are. It is enough at this point to say that the children, when they are old enough to understand, should have some actual experience with interest-bearing savings accounts.

Summary

Again, the theme is that you should know what you are doing. If you can make a list of the things for which you might well be saving, the knowledge itself is worth something. Moreover, you should know about all the kinds of saving which you are already doing: your life insurance probably includes an increase in its cash or loan value, your participation in your pension plan involves setting aside some money for the day of retirement, paying for a mortgage (not so likely for a pastor), or otherwise setting aside money—in other people's hands—for your eventual use.

In general, your minimum goal as a family must be "to be virtually debt free" and to have at least four months' salary in a savings account, or its equivalent in ready cash. Setting aside 3 to 7 percent in salary for such savings is a respectable money-saving plan for a minister receiving an average salary.

We turn now to banking, and then to insurance and investments.

Chapter 6

BANKING

In whatever town you serve, it is wise to get to know your bank and an officer in your bank. The day is gone in which banks built buildings that looked like mausoleums or Greek temples. Such a building may still stand where you live, but the old atmosphere is gone. Banks now build modern office space for themselves. They often have branches located for the convenience of the customers they must attract.

A good banker is like a good physician. The one does not recommend surgery when you don't need it. The other will not urge upon you the services you don't need at his bank. He will guide you among the choices of kinds of checking accounts, and Christmas Clubs, and savings accounts. He might suggest that you borrow from your insurance company and not from him, when it is to your advantage to do so. Indeed, the best service he can render you is the one that cannot be foreseen here because it will be a service that will meet some need that is peculiarly yours.

Moreover, the banker in your town is like other human beings: he likes to be sought out for advice. If he is a member of your congregation, and an officer who deliberates on your contract salary, your relationship is thereby changed, but probably for the better. His knowing that you take good advice, that you borrow wisely, if at all, and that you are doing what you can about saving, will make him an ally in negotiations about your salary, someday.

You can do better business if you know a little about banking before you visit the bank. Let us see whether there are some guidelines.

Upon moving to a new town, a minister should present himself at the bank, and to an officer rather than to a teller at the counter. A few discreet inquiries should tell him whom to see—the bank president if the bank is small, a vice-president otherwise. He should, of course, have an errand that goes beyond introducing himself. It will probably be to rent a safe-deposit box, to transfer his checking account from his old bank, and perhaps to do the same with a savings account. The important thing is to convey to the bank officer that here is the "new" minister, that he looks forward to a friendly connection with the bank, and that he has some sensible knowledge of banking.

Safe-deposit Box

Let's start with a safe-deposit box. A moderate-size "box" can be rented at most banks for $5 to $10 per year. This box is small and may be only 5¼" wide, 23" long, and less than 2" high. The bank keeps one key, and you another. The box, which is really a sort of drawer—among many drawers like it in the bank's vault— can be opened only when both keys are used. The bank person lets you take your box and your papers into a private cubicle, where you may put papers in and take others out. The bank is not interested in what you leave in, put in, or remove. Its only interest is that nobody but you shall have access. It is generally advisable for both husband and wife to have right of access to the safe-deposit box.

One banker points out that he and his wife have separate safe-deposit boxes, not that they are out of harmony, but in his case the system works better in the event that either he or his wife dies. His system is to have his will and his insurance policies and some of his assets in her box and vice versa. If he dies, the Government insists that the bank not let anyone remove his investments and papers from his safe-deposit box—even his wife cannot (in order to protect his estate), but his wife still has in her possession, for immediate use, his will and insurance policies. This kind of precaution is not generally needed by a minister, for the total of his and his wife's assets are usually so low that there are no inheritance taxes. In such circumstances in most states there is no problem on gaining entry into the box.

People will have different preferences about what to put under the security of a safe-deposit box. For example, some will

wish to keep casualty insurance policies there, but automobile
policies are usually not too important, for if they are lost, they are
easily replaced. On the other hand, having them with other important papers puts everything in one place, so that there is no
doubt how much coverage you have, with whom, and through what
agent. Such a consideration would be important after an accident
resulting in the unconsciousness of the person who ordinarily knows
about the policies.

Here is a full list of the items that might be put in the box.
A note is attached to a few of the items:

> Wills—husband and wife
> If you own property or a house:
>> Property deeds, title insurance policy
>> Mortgage contract
>> Mortgage payments or rent receipts
>> Property tax receipts
>
> Insurance policies:
>> Life
>> Accident and health
>> Property
>> Automobile
>
> Marriage certificate
> Birth certificates—husband, wife, children
> Passports
> Military service discharge
> Stocks, bonds, mutual fund certificates
>> NOTE: If certificates are held for you by a broker, put
>> his name and address and a list of the certificates
>> in the box.
>
> U.S. Savings Bonds
> Savings account books
> Canceled checks, bank statements
>> NOTE: Ask your banker for advice on how long to keep
>> old checks and statements. There is a limit to the
>> quantity which the box will contain and these
>> are not so important as other items.
>
> Pension plan and annuity contract
> Guarantee certificates for automobile and appliances
> Bills of sale—auto, other large items

Installment contracts

Important receipts, paid notes from borrowing

Property improvement bills

Previous income tax returns

> NOTE: Keep income tax returns and related receipts (medical bills) for five years.

School records, certificates of graduation

Naturalization papers

As has been noted, the above list would make a goodly boxful, and you must decide which items to keep at home, where fire and theft are possible, not to mention the tendency to mislay. Some items may belong at home as a matter of convenience: guarantee certificates on appliances, school records. If you retain a significant number of such items outside the safe-deposit box, try to keep them in one large envelope (tied up) at home and *not* in a filing cabinet at the church. (It is too often and too long unattended.)

Savings Account

Bank accounts fall into two categories: checking and savings. Their purposes are different from each other. Take the savings account first.

A savings account is what banks historically have provided, although they perform many other services now. You should put your money in the hands of the bank, for it isn't safe to keep such funds at home. The bank agrees to pay you a certain rate of interest, perhaps 4 percent or 5 percent—which is common as of this writing. It was once the custom to compound the interest twice each year, so that you earned interest on the interest previously earned. Later it became the practice to compound the interest monthly. Now, with computers, many banks advertise that they are, in effect, compounding interest daily. The more frequent the compounding of interest, the more your return, but not mightily.

Savings accounts are sometimes called "time deposits." That name implies that you will not be drawing out money either frequently or whimsically. It means that the bank has the right to lend your money to some other person. As a matter of current practice, banks will ordinarily give you your savings account money immediately upon demand. Most of the money put in savings accounts is lent to people and companies who are doing things with it and they cannot be expected to repay their loans upon demand. An example would be the person who is buying a house and has his mortgage with your bank. The bank has a right, therefore, *not* to return your savings account money to you when you ask for it—they could insist that you wait sixty or ninety days before they pay you. Actually, in normal times you can get it immediately and without prior notice.

Because some banks have been mismanaged and failed, the persons having checking and savings accounts in such banks lost their money. In order to protect the small savings of most citizens, the Government instituted the Federal Deposit Insurance Corporation, which now insures accounts up to a maximum of $20,000. Two cautions, therefore: do not put your money in a bank that is not covered by federal insurance; and, if you have more than $20,000 in savings, put it in more than one bank (sometimes keeping it in different accounts—each of less than $20,000—helps, but there are some legal questions on this latter technique). To be sure, in the next chapter we will see that a family having more than $20,000 on hand will probably wish to invest it to better advantage than in a savings account.

In any case, your money has optimum safety and a fairly predictable return in a savings account (the interest rate is *not* guaranteed in the future, but it probably won't change much within a year). Somewhat different from a bank, but not altogether different, is a Federal Savings and Loan Association. These so-called S & L banks are a little different from building and loan associations. They are insured by the Federal Savings and Loan Insurance Corporation, much in the same way that banks are insured by the Federal Deposit Insurance Corporation. In either case, the limit of insurance is $20,000, and you should be sure that the depository is insured and that your deposits do not exceed the insured limit. By definition, such associations or banks put more of their money into home mortgages than ordinary banks do and such associations are not allowed to handle your checking account. By contract, you do not have the right to withdraw your money at will. You have agreed that you will wait until the association has time to get its hands on the money you want. As a matter of current practice, the societies are actually giving people their money when they ask for it, but they do not have to. The interest rate is often a little higher with the savings and loan people than with a commercial bank: perhaps 5 percent when the banks are paying 4½ percent. There are differences between commercial banks, national banks, state banks, savings banks, federal savings and loan associations, building and loan associations, etc., but a minister doesn't have to be too well informed about the specialties. From a savings viewpoint, in general, the commercial bank will usually pay less interest in its savings account than a savings bank, so it pays to inquire.

If you think you can leave—indeed, should leave—your nest egg in a bank for a long period of time, you may inquire about the certificates of deposit, or CD's, sometimes called savings certificates, which some banks now offer. This is a relatively new device that tends to equalize the rates offered by commercial banks and those offered by savings institutions, but in general you do not profit from buying them unless you are willing to leave your money in these certificates for at least a year. They pay perhaps one-half to one percent more in interest than the typical savings account.

Checking Account

We turn now from savings accounts to checking accounts. Even people who say they cannot save need to have accounts upon which they can write checks. In fact, the checkbook is the key instrument in your spending patterns. If you have agreed that your wife should learn about the family's finances, she should begin by managing the checkbook. There are many jokes—of varying merit—about this topic. The joke is usually to the effect that she is unable to balance her checkbook against the bank's monthly statement. The assumption behind it all is that the bank is never wrong: it's always the lady. The truth is that with computers and other machines handling an ever-increasing flow of money and paper, banks are sometimes wrong. Every family should carefully "reconcile" its statement with the bank account and determine where the error is. There is a fair chance that your check stubs are right.

Ask your banker which kind of checking account you will need. The most expensive one is the kind where you buy a stated number of checks for a given sum of money—let us say, twenty checks for $2. That ten cents per check is the bank's fee for handling the account for you. Such an account does not require a balance of a particular size. You need only maintain enough in the account to cover the total amount of the checks you write.

Another kind requires a flat balance of perhaps $300—all the time. That $300 is available to the bank to lend its borrowers. You get no interest on it, but you also don't pay ten cents—or some other fee—for each check you write. (If you write a lot of checks each month and make many small deposits, this is the better kind of account. You should realize that you do not receive any interest on this $300, so at 5 percent you are in effect paying $15 a year or $1.25 a month for this check-writing privilege.) Still another arrangement used by some banks is a formula balance: that is to say, the bank has a formula that tells how much your minimum balance must be in the light of your account's activity. The formula serves to give the bank just enough of your money for its lending to permit it to serve your account free. If your balance is a small one and you write many checks, the bank may charge you forty cents or more for handling the extra number of items in any one month, but it is a reasonable charge for such service. Banks do charge different fees for such services, but on the whole the charges average about the same. However, check up on the type of checking account you use with your bank officer about once every three years.

A word of caution may be advisable here. Be very careful not to overdraw your account. There is almost nothing that upsets a banker more, and he seems to get just as mad about it if the amount overdrawn is ten cents or a hundred dollars. It is a very serious matter of principle to him. He thinks of it as "stealing," which in a sense it is. Of course, you think of it as humorous—just a slight miscalculation by your unmathematical wife—and easily corrected. The bank may just "give you a lecture" (it will be very gentle if the person who calls recognizes that you are a minister), but the bank may charge you a "fee" of several dollars as a penalty. If it happens twice, your banker will picture you as a happy-go-lucky mystic, a person who is irresponsible about money, and one who just doesn't keep track of his obligations. There is nothing that will get you into more trouble and reflect so adversely on your character than to sign checks that bounce. Be very careful about your checking account.

NOTE: There is a new type of checking account established by some banks called a "Cash Reserve" (or some other name) Checking Account, which establishes an amount that you can overdraw on your account—perhaps $500 or $750, depending on your income, etc. If you sign a check that overdraws your account by $195, for example, instead of bouncing your check, the bank will pay the check and automatically establish a loan for the overdrawn amount. The loan must then be paid off by making monthly fixed payments established in advance and you will be charged about 1 percent a month on the unpaid balance (an effective rate of about 12 percent a year). There is nothing wrong with such an account, but it is better to keep your accounts carefully and borrow in a more advantageous way when you need money.

There is one familiar savings plan—the so-called Christmas Club—into which savers put so many dollars or so many cents per week in order to have extra money at Christmastime. The Christmas Club offers no interest whatever (in some case, interest at a very low rate may be offered) and has none of the convenience of a checking account. In general, this type of savings is *not* recommended. If you insist on having such a savings account—which pays no interest—it shows that you just do not have any "financial sense." After reading this section, we hope you will keep your money—what little you have—working for you!

Summary

Banks perform many services. In a following chapter, we speak of investments. It is enough to say here that banks are often helpful with investments other than your bank accounts. They will purchase securities for you. They issue traveler's checks and certified checks. When you make that first visit to your new bank, you might ask for a leaflet outlining the bank's services.

For a minute you might ponder about the faith that Americans have in one another which makes check-writing possible. The whole economic system depends on it and the banks do a fantastically good job of making this simple method of exchanging funds work. It will continue to work only so long as most citizens continue to be honest. How wonderful it is that a person's name scribbled on a piece of paper can mean so much!

Chapter 7

INSURANCE

A basic insurance program will include insurance of four kinds: life, health, property, and automobile. Life insurance does not, of course, insure that you will live. Rather, it protects your family from some of the financial consequences of your death, particularly if it is untimely. By the same token, health insurance is unable to promise you good health, and fire insurance fails to stop fires. Insurance generally provides partial financial reimbursement for unforeseen or untimely calamities which could make your family's finances a disaster area. Insurance is vitally important to a good financial program.

Principles

Let us start by saying that some things are not worth insuring. To put it a different way, one should insure only against relatively big losses. You can insure against losing your fountain pen, or against cutting your finger, or against breaking your glasses—but such insurance costs you more than it is worth. You should insure only for a purpose, and when that purpose is gone the insurance should be stopped. A person can engage in a kind of self-insurance by telling himself in advance that here are certain small misfortunes which, if they occur, he will meet from his own resources. For example, to carry collision insurance on an automobile that is five years old does not make much financial sense, for you may be paying $100 or more a year for such coverage and if the car was a total loss, you might receive only $500 in benefits (the insurance company does not agree to replace the car). Though the insurance may have been wise when the car was new, the situation has changed and there is little reason to continue the insurance. Keep the fire and extended coverage and the public liability coverage but drop the collision coverage on a car after it is two or three years old.

Overinsurance

The other side of the same coin is the fact that you can't insure against every risk. It is theoretically possible to insure against every contingency that could possibly cost you money. The premiums for such insurance would add up to *more than* your income. Now, that is reducing the matter to an absurdity, but there are people who go so far along that path that they become "insurance poor." You should "self-insure" all small risks. A family should include in the annual budget the amounts needed to cover expected costs. Insurance is a costly way to pay for normal items of expense or contingencies involving relatively small losses. For example, if you know that your medical costs for the family have been averaging about $300 per year, include that amount in your budget and do not try to get reimbursed for all these expenses through insurance. Use your insurance dollar to purchase insurance for items that may exceed the $300 you have budgeted. To put it another way, if you receive a check almost every year from an insurance company for medical costs, you are probably overinsured.

By the same token, one can be underinsured. Indeed, the chances are that more Americans are insured for too little rather than too much. In many cases, the same persons are underinsured in one area and overinsured in another. The ideal, of course, would be neither too much nor too little, but the absolute ideal could be achieved only by foretelling the future, not a likely gift among ministers.

Life Insurance

In some ways, life insurance is "communal" in a thoroughly Christian sense. Let us try to understand it in this way. By observation, it was discovered that of 1,000 men age forty-two in the United States, four can be expected to die in the course of a calendar year. These thousand men could join together and promise each other that if one of their number should die, each of the 999 who continued to live would send $1 to that member's family upon notification by the secretary of the death. Each member who lives gladly makes this contribution to the family that suffered the loss; it is a sharing experience with the bereaved. The members may need to make the contribution only once or twice during the year, or if there were an epidemic or other catastrophe, they might have to send a dollar to eight or ten families in the group, though on an average, they could expect to send only $4 in the next year. An insurance company really is just such a group: the secretary, somewhat like a minister, accepts contributions from each of the members and passes them along to the bereaved or those in need. However, instead of collecting an average of $4 during the year, the insurance company collects $4.20, using the twenty cents to cover the enrollment cost of new members, postage, and other expense items. The insurance agent is the man who organizes these groups. He enrolls some people in groups that need $1,000 payments when the death occurs, some in groups that need $10,000 payments, and some that need even more. The agent not only brings the groups together originally but he represents the widows and the families too. So when he is talking to you about insurance, he can really put on a "lot of pressure," for he is talking for your wife and saying things that she would find difficult to say to you. He is providing you and your family a service that is an opportunity to share with others in their time of adversity.

If a man uses the phrase, "If anything happens to you . . . ," he probably is a life insurance salesman. He is a good citizen in his community. He is highly motivated in his work. He feels that he is performing a useful service of true social value, and his attitudes are not unlike those which motivate you in the ministry: service to others and rewards in terms of gratitude.

Most life insurance agents are carefully trained. Imagine with what care an entire industry has taught its members to employ the universal euphemism: "If anything happens to you . . ." Because he is so well trained, he recites well his company's point of view about what is best for you as to the kind of insurance you should buy, and how much. Let us see whether we can be of help in preparing you for your next interview with an insurance man.

In a very general way, there are three kinds of life insurance: term, ordinary life, and endowment insurance. All other kinds are derivatives or combinations of these three. *Term insurance* is life insurance constructed like fire insurance. With fire insurance, you get paid if you have a fire. You are paid nothing, ever, if you never have a fire. Term life insurance operates the same way: if you don't die during the term of the insurance, your family and you are paid nothing. It requires the lowest premium and in general provides the largest benefits for the least expenditure of money. *Ordinary life* is the name for life insurance policies that promise to pay something when you die, but they also provide a savings program that operates without respect to your death. This savings program is so calculated that it pays part of the higher premiums that you would normally expect to pay at the higher ages—i.e., the premium that you pay will be "level" for the whole period of your life—so you pay a little too much for the protection at the earlier ages and too little for the protection at the older ages. *Endowment insurance* combines term insurance with a savings plan so that a certain objective can be attained at a specified time, such as in twenty years, or at age sixty-five, etc. For example, if you need $4,000 twelve years from now, a $4,000 twelve-year endowment policy will provide the full $4,000 immediately upon your death if you die anytime in the next twelve years, or, if you survive, it will pay you $4,000 in cash at the end of the twelve years. In the past, insurance men have generally favored ordinary life (and its derivatives) over term insurance (in its many forms). It is true that the agent receives more in commissions for selling a $10,000 ordinary life policy than he does for selling a $10,000 term insurance policy, but this is not the reason for his pushing the more expensive policy. There are other good reasons for it that have been tested by experience.

One authority describes ordinary life in the following way (after noting that it may also be called "whole life" or "straight life"):

"A policy paying a fixed death benefit and charging a fixed premium for as many years as the holder keeps it in force. At any time before death, the policy may be cashed in for a sum specified in the contract, and the insurance will expire. This cash surrender value is in a very real sense the policyholder's own money. It is a kind of savings account that can be used as collateral for loans against the policy. It is also part of the death benefit. A $10,000 ordinary life policy with a $2,000 cash value really provides only

$8,000 of insurance protection as its death benefit. As the cash value increases (by a stated amount each year except usually the first two), the pure insurance decreases by an equal amount."

As a general rule, ministers should buy term insurance initially so as to provide the greatest protection for their families from the limited amount they can set aside for this purpose. We have seen in our chapter on banking that there are families who need the savings feature of the insurance policy to make them save at all. We will not discuss it again here, except to urge that a family that follows that course should know why it is doing what it is doing.

The important element in your interview with the salesman is your remembering what was said above in the definition of ordinary life: the part that reveals that a $10,000 benefit is only an $8,000 death benefit if $2,000 of cash value has been accumulated. Putting it another way: if a different man bought $10,000 of term insurance on the same day and at the same age as the man who bought $10,000 of ordinary life, and if they died on the same day, both families would receive $10,000 from the insurance company and nothing more. The term insurance buyer, however, would have paid a lot less in premiums and presumably could have invested the difference in premiums between ordinary life and the term policy so that the accumulated fund might be worth $2,000 the day of his death. If so, his family has $12,000—$2,000 of savings and $10,000 of death benefit. If you will remember that little, oversimplified exercise in arithmetic, you will be a wiser insurance buyer. As a practical matter, the advantages of the term insurance plus an investment program are considerable for the earlier years, but they are often negligible over periods of twenty years or more.

Let us describe some of the kinds of term insurance. *Five-year renewable term* is a policy promising to pay a fixed death benefit for a premium that stays level for the first five years and it is renewable at the end of four years for another five-year period and this option continues to be repeated up to about age sixty. The price goes up with each five-year renewal, because the man is that much closer to death. One must pass a medical examination at the beginning, but not at renewal. This policy can be changed at any time—at a higher premium—to an ordinary life policy for an amount equal to or less than the face value of the original term insurance.

Decreasing term is the name for term insurance in which the premium stays the same each year, but the death benefit decreases each year. The merit here is that since you did not die and leave your family without income last year, therefore presumably the amount of insurance needed has been reduced. As you get older, the amount of insurance you need may be reduced. For example, your children may have matured and become self-supporting or your own savings plans have had time to accumulate substantial amounts, etc. This type of insurance can also be used effectively to assure a specified objective, e.g., you are paying off an indebtedness gradually—perhaps a mortgage—and if you should die, the insurance will be just enough to pay off the balance of the indebtedness, thus freeing your wife from further payments.

A *family income* plan is really a decreasing term insurance policy. It guarantees a fixed monthly income for a stated period of time. The period might be from the day you bought the policy till the day your youngest child finishes college. Every month you live is a month subtracted from the number of months of income which the insurance company may have to pay out. If you die at any point in the agreed term, the company pays from that month until the end of the term. Since this is an especially good type of insurance for a minister's family, it is described in more detail in the following paragraph. (Not all insurance companies call this type of coverage "family income," but the insurance agent will know and recognize what you want).

Let us assume that a minister has purchased a $10,000 ordinary life policy shortly after his marriage, and later when a child is born, he wants to increase the amount of insurance he is carrying. He approaches the insurance company and asks them for a *twenty-year* family income policy as an addition to his basic ordinary life policy. This addition provides that if he dies immediately, his wife would be paid $100 a month for twenty years and then the full $10,000 would be paid to his wife in addition (his child would be twenty-one at that time and probably in college). Note that if the minister died immediately after buying the family income policy, his widow would receive 20 times $1,200, plus $10,000, or $34,000 in benefits; if he died one year later, she would receive 19 times $1,200, plus $10,000, or $32,800 in benefits, etc., the amount of insurance decreasing $1,200 each year over a twenty-year period and then the original $10,000 would remain at the original premium rate. (The cost of the additional insurance would terminate at the end of twenty years.) The cost of the original $10,000 of ordinary life for a minister at age twenty-eight would be $136 per year in one company and the cost of the additional family income policy if taken at age twenty-nine would be $40 per year if taken in the same company. He would be buying much more protection ($34,000 versus $10,000) at a cost of only 30 percent more in premiums. (NOTE: Most companies also issue a *fifteen-year* family income plan which would be more suitable in some instances depending on the age of the children at the time of purchase.) The reason these plans are emphasized is that they often provide the most insurance for the least cost. They are cheaper than the usual term insurance, since they are attached to an ordinary life policy and that policy absorbs some of the administrative costs.

We have already recommended that ministers take term insurance initially rather than ordinary life. A second recommendation would be that the minister who has purchased ordinary life insurance should have a family income plan added to the ordinary life policy if he needs more protection. Thus, he has his enforced savings program, plus a planned element of pure death protection.

Added Values

Life insurance has some added values, not ordinarily available when money is invested in other ways. For example, life insurance proceeds paid out at death have a tax-favored status. The entire amount usually escapes federal tax, and in most states there is no tax on insurance proceeds paid to a named beneficiary. At the time of death there is no delay, no red tape, and there are no court costs in getting the money into the hands of the beneficiary.

As to the taxes, the policies with cash values have discernible advantages. As they increase in value, the interest on the invested portion of the money is not taxed as current income. Also, if you take the proceeds at maturity as an annuity to be paid over your remaining lifetime, you will pay taxes only on the increased value, but under favorable annuity tax rules. The insurance companies tell you exactly how much in taxes you will need to pay each year.

Costs

The true actual cost of insurance is not easily determined even by an insurance agent. If one company was demonstrably much lower in cost than another, the agents would all try to be agents for that company, since it would be easier to sell those policies. Some companies offer services that do cost a little but that are worth much to the policyholder, and good advice may save much more than the savings of a few cents per year per one thousand dollars of insurance. There are published books that compare, in a very rough way, the cost of insurance purchased from several hundred of the better known life insurance companies in the United States. (There are over 1,500 life insurance companies currently doing business.) All such comparisons are for "past" costs and in the future the costs can change materially among companies. For this reason, a minister will not profit greatly from studying such cost histories, for his real concern is not in what the companies did in the past but how they will operate in the next fifty years. Even the experts (the actuaries) do not place their insurance with the same companies.

It is important that you select the company carefully at the outset, and once you have made the selection, it is generally better to stay with that company for that insurance amount or policy. In general, do not buy from an insurance agent who suggests that you drop a former policy and buy a better one with his company. If you need additional insurance or wish to replace a policy that is terminating, it is entirely proper to buy from a different company, but usually it is best to ask the company with which you have the policy to help you attain a different objective and then compare costs before you change.

It is possible to buy life insurance at a flat guaranteed premium that never changes. This is called "nonparticipating" insurance, and it can be obtained from such large companies as Travelers, Aetna Life, Occidental Life, Connecticut General, Lincoln National, and many others. This type of insurance is preferred in Europe, but in the United States most insurance (about 55 percent) is purchased on a "participating" basis from "mutual" life insurance companies. On the whole, the mutual or participating companies charge more for the insurance initially, but through the payment of dividends, the net cost is often less in the long run. Most of the other companies with which ministers might be familiar are mutual companies, though their names are not descriptive. Some of the larger mutual companies are: Metropolitan, Prudential, Equitable, New York Life, Mutual of New York, Northwestern Mutual, Connecticut Mutual, John Hancock, New England, Massachusetts Mutual, Mutual Benefit.

No matter what life insurance policy you buy, no matter from whom you buy it, it is recommended that you pay the premiums annually. In fact, they are due annually, as of the beginning of the policy year. If at the beginning of the policy year you pay only one quarter of the annual premium, in effect the insurance company is lending you the other three quarters at interest. To pay monthly is to borrow eleven twelfths of the annual premium at interest. Pay annually or you commit yourself to a lifetime of silent borrowing toward your insurance premiums.

As a matter of interest, Chart E gives the "nonparticipating" costs of several types of insurance at various ages charged by one insurance company. The premium for such policies purchased from a mutual company would probably be more, but you would receive dividends to reduce the costs to those shown or possibly a little lower.

CHART E

ANNUAL PREMIUMS (Nonparticipating)

Per $1,000 of Original Insurance

Age at Time of Purchase	5-Year Term	Ordinary Life	20-Year Family Income (Special Term)	20-Year Endowment
25	$4.33	$12.35	$3.51	$41.69
30	4.41	14.65	4.21	42.01
35	5.04	17.61	5.86	42.63
40	6.61	21.55	8.30	43.76
45	9.08	26.58	12.21	45.67
50	13.40	32.61	18.93	48.65
55	20.05	40.57	27.98	53.14
60	32.03	51.71	41.64	60.26

Annuities

Once we introduce the word "annuity" into our discussion, we are talking about retirement, and that means it is time for the minister to take a look at the pension and insurance plan of his church. It is time also to ponder Social Security. It is not unusual for a church pension plan to provide substantial insurance benefits payable at the death of a minister, e.g., a widow's pension, a salary continuation benefit for a year, children's education or college benefits, payments to minor children to the age of twenty-one, etc. These benefits are paid for specific purposes, but they are, in effect, "life insurance" carried on the life of the minister and represent a value of perhaps $5,000 to $50,000, depending upon the denomination to which he belongs. To say it in a different way, it might take perhaps $45,000 of life insurance to provide the benefits promised under the church program, so the minister needs to know what these benefits are in order to determine how much additional insurance he needs to buy. Similarly, the benefits paid to the members of the family of a deceased minister may very easily exceed $80,000 under the Government's Social Security program. These amounts are in addition to the minister's own retirement pension, so they must be considered in connection with the insurance program. In our next chapter, we will look at the retirement provisions of Social Security and a typical church pension plan. Meanwhile, we must look at them as death benefit functions.

Beyond a church pension plan, and beyond Social Security, there is the fact that life insurance companies sell annuities. You pay so much a month, or a year, as premiums, until an agreed age. At that age, the annuity hourglass is turned upside down and the insurance company begins to pay you back. (You can also pay a single premium of $1,000 or more and arrange to have the annuity start immediately or at some future date.) Usually, the annuity will go to the end of your life, no matter how long. If you die too soon after starting to collect, you can arrange for your heirs to get the difference between the dollars you put in and the dollars you received.

Annuities can be tied to two lives. Annuities can be bought in a lump sum—at retirement, for instance—by putting the contents of a savings account into the annuity. Or, a matured or discontinued life insurance policy can be changed into an annuity, and probably should.

NOTE: If an active minister wishes to purchase additional annuities, he should consult an informed life insurance agent about the advantages of a "tax sheltered" annuity—for which he is eligible because he is a minister.

How Much

Or, coming at it another way, we may ask how much life insurance any man needs, considering that he has Social Security and a church pension plan with death benefits. The rule of thumb of at least two or three times the annual salary is not really meaningful. Chart F shows what Rev. Mr. Smith did when he decided it was necessary to review the family's insurance program. It took him a little longer than he expected, but when he got through he was pleasantly surprised about the provisions that had been made. Actually the process of thinking it through and talking frankly with his wife about the whole program gave him an assurance he had not felt before. Somehow the worries that he had tried to suppress over the past years now disappeared.

CHART F

MR. SMITH'S LIFE INSURANCE PROGRAM

Rev. A. B. Smith, wanting to review his life insurance program on his thirty-seventh birthday, noted that his wife was now age thirty-five, his daughter, Gail, seven, and his son, John, five, and that he was currently receiving a salary of $8,000 plus parsonage. His salary had averaged about $6,000 per year over the ten-year period since he was ordained and began service to the church. After studying his church pension plan and some recent folders on Social Security, he was able to list the following benefits which his family would receive "if something happened to him."

Wife's Benefits   °$ 430   a year from church beginning immed-
  (age 35)   iately for life

                    °$ 1,080   a year from Social Security for 13 years
                                 until youngest child attains age 18, i.e.,
                                 to age 48

                    No Social Security benefits from age 49 to age 62.
                                 (Mrs. Smith could get a reduced benefit
                                 at age 60.)

                     $ 1,188   a year beginning at age 62 for life from
                                 Social Security

                     $ 8,900   as a Salary Continuation payable
                                 monthly for 12 months (one year's
                                 salary = $8,000 plus value of parsonage)

Some other payments under a medical plan which
would pay perhaps 65% of his medical expenses
incurred just prior to his death.

                     $10,000   lump-sum payment by "X" Insurance
                                 Company under an ordinary life policy.

Gail   °$ 1,080   per year under Social Security to age 22.
  (age 7)   (It was assumed that she would gradu-
                                 ate from high school at age 18 and
                                 from college at age 22.)

                     $ 200   per year under church pension plan to
                                 age 21

                     $ 1,000   a year for each of four years in college
                                 from church insurance program

John   °$ 1,080   per year under Social Security to age 22.
  (age 5)   (It was assumed that he would graduate
                                 from high school at age 18 and from
                                 college at age 22.)

                     $ 200   per year under church pension plan to
                                 age 21

                     $ 1,000   a year for each of four years in college
                                 from church insurance program

° Mr. Smith discovered that he couldn't determine these himself,
for he had no record of the salary on which his pension dues had
been paid over the past ten years, and though he knew that he
had paid Social Security taxes on the maximum amount each
year, he couldn't remember what the maximums were (since
they had been changed several times). Fortunately, he had just
received information from the church pension plan telling him
what his credits were and he called the local Social Security
office and determined what they thought he might receive (subject to confirmation later based on his actual payments).

Mr. Smith then summarized the preceding in the following table.

Family Income

(The year before his death it would have been $8,000 plus parsonage.)

Year After Death	Wife's Age	Total Income	Year After Death	Wife's Age	Total Income
1st	35	$22,970	14th	48	$4,990
2d-12th	36-46	4,070	15th	49	4,990
12th	46	5,070	16th	50	2,710
13th	47	5,070	17th	51	2,710
			18th-27th	52-61	430
			27th & over	62 & over	1,618

Mr. Smith was surprised at how uneven the income was going to be, and after discussion with his wife and later with an insurance agent, he rearranged his insurance program. Mrs. Smith thought she would reenter the teaching field but discovered that she would need a one-year refresher course at the university to obtain a teacher's certificate in the state in which the family would live (she planned to live near her parents). She would need $1,200 to clear up local bills, $400 of the funeral expenses (as she hoped the church would pay the balance of the funeral costs), $950 to move the furniture to an apartment in a city 800 miles away, $4,000 for the one year at the university (if her parents did a fair share of the baby-sitting), but she wouldn't be able to do that until John was in school on a full schedule basis two years hence. The plan was to be flexible so that it could be changed—since Mrs. Smith would be able to manage the money and not lose it. The college years for the children were the years that worried him most, and also that low-income period for his wife between ages 49 and 62, but it was hoped she could earn enough money teaching to support herself and have some extra for the children.

Anybody who tries to specify the exact amount of insurance another man should buy is attempting the impossible. There are, however, some sentences that may be written, tested for common sense, and modified by any known factors in an individual family. It is a certainty that some things are out of the question, such as buying enough insurance at a young age to continue your salary to the date when it would in any case have ceased by reason of retirement. For example, our seminary graduate of twenty-seven wants to work forty years, or until he is sixty-seven. We have arranged for him to die at thirty-seven, at a time when his income is $9,000 per year. When he dies, he has thirty years of income not earned, and thirty times $9,000 is $270,000. Indeed, if he buys the policy to provide full future income at age twenty-seven (when he is probably at his "poorest" economic level), he must multiply an average salary of perhaps $8,000 by forty to arrive at $320,000 as the amount of salary his family might lose by his death. Although it would only take a capital fund of $158,344 at 4 percent interest to provide $8,000 a year for forty years, still that much insurance is not reasonable.

Next, we are able to note that the death of a male head of the household reduces the expenses of the family by about 25 percent or 35 percent. That is to say, with you "gone" your family could maintain its present standard of living with about 65 percent or 75 percent of the income you are now using. Part of the reason for that is that the kinds of income they get after you die tend not to be taxable. Once we have established that range of percentages, we should introduce into our vocabulary, and emphasize throughout, the word *until*. We should look to a combination of pension benefits, Social Security benefits, available savings, and life insurance that will maintain something like 65 percent or 75 percent of your income *until*: until something. Until the family moves out of the parsonage and gets reestablished in its "new" home. Until the surviving wife (and mother) is retrained for entry or reentry into the labor force. Until the son who is studying engineering is finished studying, can support himself, and perhaps spare something for his mother. Until your widow attains age sixty-two and Social Security begins its widow's pension. The "untils" are very difficult to solve adequately even with insurance. Clearly, a standard consideration would be income for the family until the last child finishes college. If that is going to be eight years after the father dies, we have two distinct situations within the eight years. While one child is in college, the last child may need the mother at home, preferably not working, or not working too much, and the next to the last child needs his tuition bills paid. When the last child enters college, and it may well be while the next to the last is still a student, there would be two tuition bills to pay, but the mother has minimal motherhood responsibilities at home, for the children are gone. Thus, she is available for employment, but perhaps she needs a year of training for employment, in which case there will be three tuition bills to pay. When, however, the last child finishes college, and the mother is gainfully employed, there is minimal need for insurance resources, if indeed any need at all. That is what we mean by *until:* insurance cannot buy a fatherless family a financial future at all like the one he, alive, would have provided. It can, and should, absorb the collisionlike financial shock of his death, and provide for the measures that must be taken to "secure the ship."

One church's pension plan provides for the continuation of the man's salary for an entire year (there is, however, a limit of $10,000 on the amount), and that is probably the best life insurance a minister can have. It assures that the family can go on living as they were, or that they can cut back expenditures and save some of the salary payments for the period beyond the year. Most important, it relieves them of the necessity for planning the future in haste. If your church does not have this feature in its pension plan, you should include it in your own life insurance program.

It must be realized, in thinking about insurance against the death of the husband, that his wife may remarry. The earlier the age at which he dies, the more likely that she will remarry. This is perhaps not a proper subject for these pages on finance. It is an extremely private matter, but the minister and his wife should discuss it. The fact is that a minister who does not want his wife to work or to remarry after his death has an obligation to carry a very substantial amount of insurance. At the same time, he is not relieved of all responsibility should he take the position that she should remarry, for it isn't easy to remarry and especially so if she is "saddled" with two or three children who have their father's characteristics!

The Wife

A more appropriate topic would be job training for a wife whose husband is very much alive. If you have married a secretary, a nurse, or a teacher, she has an asset that can eliminate thousands of dollars from your insurance program. There is nothing special about those three professions that demeans any other profession, except that they come quickly to mind as examples of training in constant demand. You belong to a level of society where culture is an insistent factor. That being the case, there is a good chance that your wife—and alas, your potential widow—is a well-educated lady, interested in painting or music or the other arts, but not really prepared to fill the jobs that appear in the Sunday's want-ad pages. Whatever she is doing with her time now, and heaven knows she hasn't any to waste, you might together ponder whether any of it leads to gainful employment, should it ever become necessary. Will she need a one-year refresher course to get a teacher's certificate? or regain her skills long unused? or learn something new? Cost: $4,000?

The Family

A few more sentences and we shall be finished with life insurance. What about insurance for the wife and mother of the family? It has been argued that a family needs substantial protection against the loss of its full-time housewife, that the employment of a housekeeper is such a formidable expense (if one can be found) that the death of a wife and mother would put the family in an impossible position. It does! And sometimes it forces the minister into remarriage earlier than his parishioners think proper. However, if money is scarce and the insurance program minimal, place all the insurance dollars on the life of the wage earner and none on the wife or on the children. The cost of burial should be minimal for a minister and should be "budgetable" for members of his family.

The treatment above of the matter of insurance for a wife underscores the nature of this discussion of insurance. There is almost no "room for emotion" in a sensible discussion of insurance. It is simply a device to hedge against a financial catastrophe. There are enough real disasters and problems without our conjuring up false ones and then insuring against them. Life insurance is one way of joining a group so as to assure that a particular financial goal is attained—whether you live or die—and at a cost of less than the normal rate of interest. It is akin to writing a Christian will, for it forces one to think of others when we are no longer here to help.

Health Insurance

Health insurance is not dissimilar to life insurance in that its purpose is to offset some of the financial results of the frailty of the human body. In its simplest form, it meets medical and hospital bills. It is most widely sold by organizations known as Blue Cross and Blue Shield, the former paying hospital bills and the latter paying for physicians' or surgeons' services. (NOTE: Blue Cross and Blue Shield coverage is usually sold to groups at better rates than to individuals. Your ecclesiastical body or the local council of churches should be providing the group opportunity to ministers in the same way as a business firm might offer such a group plan to its employees.) The local organizations that bear those two names vary as to what they will provide and as to what they charge. They are ordinarily founded by public-spirited people and most hospitals and physicians join in offering the services they provide. In most communities, Blue Cross and Blue Shield offer good insurance coverage at reasonable cost (even though it may seem high to you!). In a few areas, there are hospitals that give ministers and sometimes their families as much as a 50 percent discount on their bills—and in such instances a policy with a commercial insurer might be preferable to standard Blue Cross coverage. Occasionally, a private or commercial insurance company has a better plan which will suit your particular needs, but be sure you are comparing like things when you compare. A most important feature has to do with cancellation: if a policy is going to be canceled—as if in reprisal—the first time you make a claim, you are insured with the wrong company!

Accident and Health Insurance

A more expensive form of insurance, usually called accident and health insurance, provides for weekly payments to anyone who is ill or injured after a waiting period usually of three to seven days. One way of looking at such coverage is that it provides income while you are "off the job." Another viewpoint is that such benefits will pay you more or less the kind of money you will probably owe the hospital and the doctors. Before you buy accident and health insurance, you should determine the congregation's (or your employer's) attitude about the continuation of your salary if you were to be ill for several months. If you believe—or know—that they would continue your salary for as much as six months, then your insurance should be adjusted accordingly.

Next, you should know whether your denominational pension or insurance program provides major medical coverage. Some denominations have plans that deal with all medical expenses above a certain deductible—such as $50 or $100 per illness—while other plans have large deductibles such as 5 percent of annual salary. Of the expenses over the deductible, the major medical plan often pays 80 percent and you—or perhaps a generous employer or congregation—pay 20 percent. Such coverage determines what supplemental protection you need, if any. Remember the advice: Insure only against large losses and accept the risk of the smaller items of cost yourself. It is much cheaper and better in the long run to self-insure all risks which, if they occurred, you could pay for by an adjustment in your budget over a period of one or two years.

Health insurance is often advertised in magazines and by direct mail. If the companies are licensed to do business in your state, your state's insurance commissioner has some degree of control and regulation. If they are not licensed there, he is powerless to protect you. In general, you will be well advised to stick with good, well-known insurance companies. They can and do provide coverage equal to or better than any you will find advertised in these special ways. (An insurance company can sell insurance in any state by mail, so you will need to inquire about its license to do business in your state. Remember, too, that someday you may move to another state.) Determine what you want and need. Then buy it from a good company at standard rates and you will be better off in the long run. (The fine print in an insurance contract is very tricky reading. It takes an expert to know what is excluded or "not covered," especially in health or accident policies.)

Property Insurance

Property insurance on a house and its contents is less important, of course, for the manse dweller than for the person who buys a house. If you have a house and it is mortgaged, the mortgagor will have seen to it that you have at least enough fire insurance coverage to cover his mortgage. In addition, you should consider a comprehensive property owner's policy, sometimes a homeowner or household policy that covers fire, theft, storm damage, vandalism, the contents and furniture of the house as well as the house, and even gives certain protections to items you take with you on journeys.

Make sure that your coverage is high enough to reimburse you for the current value of your house. A mortgage holder may insist on only enough coverage to pay off the mortgage—which may be only 60 percent of its value—but you are interested in protecting the full current value of the house. An offsetting consideration: subtract from the presumed sale value of the property the value of the land, for the value of the ground itself will not be destroyed even if the house is a total loss—and it is unlikely that anyone can steal the lot!

Inventories

Whether you live in a manse or a house of your own, you should buy some insurance on the household contents—furniture, rugs, beds, refrigerator, piano, etc. The insurance people recommend—but almost nobody does it—that you "inventory" your household goods; that is, that you make a list of everything in the house, giving some estimate of its depreciated value. Then, after a totally destructive fire, you have a list from which to make your claims for reimbursement. (NOTE: There is no point to making the list and then leaving it in the house where it may burn up with the contents. Keep it at the church or in the bank's safe-deposit box.) Short of a complete inventory, you might try the following: look at your insurance policy and see the amount for which the household things are insured. Then speculate on the cost of replacing the items in the living room. You may have to turn off the television for a half hour, but it will be worth it to guess what it would cost to replace: this chair, that sofa, the rug, all the pictures, the TV, a hassock, and a multitude of items you forget you have, but know you need. You may get the idea that your amount of insurance is not enough and the exercise will be valuable.

If you have some especially valuable items, you had better record that fact with the insurance company. For example, if you are a moderate-income family but have inherited a $3,500 diamond ring, you couldn't blame the insurance company for wondering whether you really owned anything so valuable before the fire. There are rugs of surprising value, too, and the company should know about them before there is trouble.

Special Coverages

A "floater" clause in your contract usually insures your household things—for a total up to 10 percent of the face value of all the contents—while you have them with you on a journey. It's difficult to collect insurance for cash you might claim to have been stolen, but the theft of your clothing or their loss by fire in the car or in a motel is covered. Be sure you have a floater clause, because the exposure to this hazard and to the unusual is increased when you are traveling or just taking a day in the country or at the shore.

When you are planning to move, be sure to tell your insurance company before you move. If they are insuring you at a certain rate because you are in a brick house near a fire hydrant and a city fire department, they will not want to provide the same insurance at the same rates when you move to a frame house in an area where there is only a volunteer fire department, for example. Moreover, furniture moved from your residence to a storage company warehouse is no longer covered, unless you have arranged for it. If you do move, arrange for insurance while your things are in transit. The amount of insurance automatically carried by the mover for you is altogether inadequate and it will probably be cheaper for you to arrange the extra insurance with your insurance company than through the mover's insurance company.

Public Liability

If you live in a house owned by the church, be sure you (or the church) carry some "public liability" on the house and grounds (as well as on the church building and grounds). It may cost only ten to fifteen dollars a year and can be important. As examples: (1) Your young son leaves his bicycle on the sidewalk, and an elderly woman walks by at night, fails to see it, falls and breaks her hip—a suit could involve $5,000 or more. (2) You leave the garage door open for a short period. While you are out, a neighborhood child (whom you have repeatedly lectured on staying off your property) walks over, sees a can of paint on a shelf, tries to get it off with a stick, the paint can falls, hits him in the eye, and he loses it. You lose a suit because you left the door open and the paint can was determined to be an "attractive nuisance," so it was your fault. Cost: $22,000.

Automobile Insurance

Automobile insurance is a costly part of the maintenance of an automobile or automobiles. Early in this chapter, to illustrate the concept of self-insurance, we said that you should probably not carry collision insurance on a car over two years old—certainly not on a car over three years old—because the depreciation in the first few years is enormous. Collision insurance is the type of insurance that guarantees that after an accident which you could not successfully blame on someone else (such as overturning on a slippery road, or going to sleep at the wheel, or backing into a tree, etc.), your car would be restored to its former condition, or replaced with a sum of money equal to the book value of that kind of automobile at that age. We are saying that you should carry collision only during the first two years of the life of your automobile, if at all. Look at the premiums you pay for collision insurance. Ponder how many years of going without an accident you would need in order to be able to pay, from premiums not paid, the cost of the first extensive accident. That is what the insurance company has done. It is what you should do. (The individual who buys a car with a little down and monthly payments is forced to buy collision insurance—even if the car is secondhand—so such persons pay not only considerable in interest but substantial amounts in extra insurance costs.)

The important kind of automobile insurance for a minister is public liability and property damage. You should buy it with limits of at least $25,000 and $50,000, which would mean that the insurance company would pay, if you were successfully sued, as much as $25,000 for the injuries or death of any one person, and as much as $50,000 for the injuries or death of all those whom you harmed in any one accident.

NOTE: It is surprising how many ministers carry very low limits of coverage. To many laymen, this seems to imply that the minister doesn't value human life very highly. The cost of the higher limits is very little more and strongly recommended. It would be far better, in a time of huge awards by juries in accident cases, to have limits of $100,000 and $300,000. You simply must not drive on the streets or highways without this kind of insurance, and you must not permit your children to do so.

An example may not be amiss. Let us say you obtained a personal liability contract with a so-called cut-rate insurance company and took a chance on $10,000 of public liability coverage. You had an accident, which was clearly your fault, killed a few people, and were sued for $200,000. The insurance company, after reviewing the situation, might come to the conclusion that they could not win the case in court, so in order to save legal fees, etc., they would simply agree to pay the $10,000 and step out of the case. This would leave the problem with you and you would need to obtain your own lawyer, pay large legal fees, and even then a jury might award damages of $100,000. This judgment would follow you wherever you might serve in a different state, and the obligation would keep you and your family poor "forever." (Had you been insured for a decent amount in a good company for a few dollars more per year, they probably would have fought the case for you. As it was, you tried to "get by" and must pay for the chance you took.) Ministers were generally immune from such suits in the past, but this is no longer true.

A comprehensive clause in an automobile policy, usually referred to as an "extended coverage," will pay for damages to your car, other than those caused by collision, for a variety of reasons. The list of possible occurrences is impressive: breakage of glass, loss caused by missiles, falling objects, fire, theft or larceny, explosion, earthquake, windstorm, hail, water, flood, malicious mischief or vandalism, riot or civil commotion, and colliding with a bird or an animal. It also covers your personal effects within the car against fire and lightning losses. This is a "must" coverage and it doesn't cost much.

A small premium will cover damages or harm done by an uninsured motorist. It is recommended that you buy it. Some states require that you buy it if you buy insurance at all. It covers damage to your automobile or your person by a driver whom you could successfully sue if he had any insurance or assets to pay the amount of your judgment against him. If he was not insured, and you are unable to collect the damages he owes you, your insurance company will step into the picture and pay the costs. The premium is about two dollars a year.

Towing is a separate item in some policies and usually promises to pay $15 or $25 each time your automobile is disabled and must be towed. Some auto policies include it without an additional charge. Be sure you know what you are entitled to, i.e., *read* your policy. (Your wife may want this coverage more than you do.) Some ministers believe it is better to buy this coverage as part of a membership in an automobile club (if there is one that services your area). Perhaps your community responsibilities suggest that you should support your local auto club. For another, the road service of the club covers such things as changing tires and starting cold engines. Either way, it is a relatively minor expense. Such coverage or membership is not necessary, but it is nice if you can afford it. Through the automobile club you can obtain good auto insurance, and if you get into trouble, it will assist you (often the automobile club is a great help when you are trying to collect from another fellow's insurance company!). It is very important to obtain your auto coverage from a good company—one that will not cancel when you attain age sixty-five, one with which you can continue to deal when you move to another state, and one that will pay legitimate claims promptly and one that will fight illegitimate claims. Some "shyster" companies virtually decline all claims and force the claimant to take court action before they are willing to settle. Remember that you want protection, but as a responsible person you also want others to be paid if the accident is your fault. So be careful in selecting your company, and if you are currently insured in the wrong company, change before it is too late at the next policy anniversary.

In an earlier chapter we talked about companies that cancel summarily the policies of persons who have accidents or several moving traffic violations. The companies claim to be losing money on their automobile business, and are trying to keep only the "better risks" on their rolls. A few years ago it would have been possible to recommend a number of substantial companies as being unlikely to cancel your insurance except under the most grievous circumstances. Because the different states have limited increases in rates while the claim rates and awards have been increasing

rapidly, most casualty companies have been losing money on their
automobile business for years. Currently, even the older more re-
liable companies have found it necessary to check new applicants
very carefully—especially if there are teen-age drivers in the family. Now, all companies seem to have computers. The state highway patrols have computers, and when they run their tapes
together they have a complete rundown on you and your family:
convictions, summonses, teen-age drivers, claims for collisions, etc.

You should be warned also against some of the newer companies that have a reputation of canceling after the first claim is
made. If you aren't sure that you are getting the best insurance
bargain, and you see television and other advertisements for something a lot cheaper, beware. It is best to get your insurance in an
old established company with a good reputation and national coverage. The basic test is not the premium but how they settle their
claims: Are they reasonable, fair, prompt, and careful? Among
those companies which have such a reputation one would include
Travelers, Aetna, Federal, Insurance Company of North America,
Liberty Mutual, companies used by automobile clubs (AAA), and
many others.

Deductibles

In all insurance buying, don't forget that the company has
figured how much it must receive in premiums to cover all the
troubles that are going to befall its customers. In addition, it must
meet the expenses of being an insurance company, and it must
stay solvent. That means it must take in more money than the
people's troubles add up to. In turn, that means that it is a good
idea not to pay for insurance in any case where you could afford
the risk yourself. We are talking about self-insurance again, and
one of its most desirable forms is in "deductible" clauses. Collision
insurance, for example, is sold with deductible clauses of, for example, $100, which means you pay the first one hundred dollars
of the cost of any collision. You pay the full cost, of course, of
any incident costing less than $100. If you must buy collision
insurance, we recommend a deductible clause of at least $100.
(You can get coverage with a deductible of $250 or more.) The
more deductible you have, the more nearly you are self-insured.
The companies give you a big break on premiums if you share in

the cost of the big accidents and pay all the costs of the little ones. Apart from the fact that their liability is reduced, there is the fact that it costs money to settle a claim: somebody has to come see the damages, perhaps he must haggle with you or with the garage, and there are forms to fill out and file. It costs them just as much to settle a $100 claim as a $500 claim, so by reducing the number of claims they can save a considerable amount in expenses. Deductibles reduce the number of claims!

Travel Accident Insurance

If you buy travel accident insurance, be sure it covers automobile accidents, for that is where the risk is. Perhaps the least valuable policy you can buy is the one at the airport counter where for a few dollars you can buy a few hundred thousand dollars of coverage against the loss of your life during one round trip. Airplane travel is statistically so safe that one ventures to say it would be fiscally more prudent to play the slot machines than to play insurance policy machines at the airport. In general, we recommend against a minister spending any of his money on travel accident insurance and in favor of spending the extra money for more life insurance.

The fact is that the chances of your dying as the result of an accident are only 10 percent. To express it another way, if you die, the chances are 90 percent that you will *not* die because of an accident. The chances of your dying on a single plane trip are miniscule. And if you happen to die on such a trip, remember that it is the cheapest and quickest way you could possibly die. Why should you insure against dying the cheapest way? What reasonable explanation could you give for insisting that your wife receive $40,000 if you die that way and failing to provide anything special for her if you die slowly and leave a medical bill of $5,000 for her to pay in addition? Since you are an American, you will probably insist on buying accident insurance—despite this advice—but if you do, at least buy it by the year and not by the trip. You can get full accident coverage for about $1 to $2 a year for each $1,000 of coverage and it will pay off for 'any accident— car, plane, bus, falling in the bathtub, skiing, etc.—whenever and wherever it occurs, even in an airplane and anyplace in the world.

Yes, it is very cheap because it doesn't provide much protection really!

Summary

Some general rules about all insurance: know with whom you are dealing, use reason and not your emotions, self-insure all that you can, challenge every presupposition, and don't be superstitious about it!

Insurance is not a "fun" topic. It deals with possible disasters! If you have the good fortune in life never to receive a benefit on your life, health, or property insurance, you should be thankful. You will have contributed your money to those who suffered the disasters, and generally speaking, this is a good way to spend some of your money.

Chapter 8

INVESTMENTS

Having looked at banking, we turn to investments. We should remember, however, that the savings accounts discussed in an earlier chapter are investments too. Indeed, a savings account is the typical family way of putting money aside for future use, and earning income on it. All other forms of investment may be measured in terms of the savings account, using it as a benchmark.

For example, the money in a savings account is exceptionally secure since a Federal Government insurance program covers it. The interest rate is published, and virtually assured. You must ask yourself whether any other investment you contemplate will be as safe as a savings account. In most cases, the answer will be, "No, it isn't as safe, but then the return, or the hope of return, is greater, and worth the extra risk." You must balance these two offsetting factors in your mind—and in your conversations between man and wife, or with a banker or stockbroker.

Government Bonds

As of this writing, a savings account, or a bank's certificate of deposit, will produce more revenue than the Federal Government's E Bonds. The E Bond yields 5.50 percent interest if you hold it for a full five years and ten months and then continues to yield that rate if you keep it beyond the full term. You must compare the rate with the 5 percent to 6 percent generally paid by banks and savings and loan institutions.

Apart from patriotism—and that is not our present topic—it is difficult to urge upon families the widespread holding of Government E Bonds, unless they are issued to yield a higher return.

They sometimes make attractive gifts, because they can be bought in small amounts, have tangible value, and will provide an occasion for remembering again the giver, on the day the donee cashes them in. (NOTE: The U.S. Government issues many types of bonds—long term and short term—usually at lower interest rates than paid on industrial and utility bonds. The E Bonds were especially designed for the small investor—most of the others are in $1,000 units.)

Another aspect of both savings accounts and Government E Bonds is that they never pay back more than the amount you put into them originally, except that they pay interest: the savings accounts at regular intervals, the E Bonds at maturity. The $75 you pay for an E Bond yields 5.50 percent interest if held to maturity. The bond can then be redeemed for $100. Another investment having similar characteristics is a "bond" usually issued by a railroad, a large industrial firm, or a utility. Such bonds have a prescribed life-span and pay a specific interest rate.

Bonds

Usually, bonds are considered relatively safe investments. This is because they have a kind of first claim on all the assets of the company if it should go broke. Of course, you may consider it is a little farfetched to think about the bankruptcy of a large company in which you might have a bond, but it does happen and is happening every day. We hope it will not be your company that goes out of business, but you must think in those terms when you invest.

Ratings

Only bonds of a good company are "safe." You can purchase bonds in poor companies and some of these bonds are more speculative than most stocks. Most bonds are given "ratings" by certain rating companies, such as Standard & Poor's or Moody's. A triple A (i.e., AAA) rating is tops, using Standard & Poor's classifications, so a triple A bond is the best and safest you can buy. A double A bond is next safest, and the ratings go on down, AAA, AA, A, BBB, BB, B, etc. The corresponding classifications by Moody's are: Aaa, Aa, A, Baa, Ba, etc. The lower the bond is rated, usually the higher the interest that is paid, i.e., a B bond may pay 1 percent or 2 percent more interest each year than a triple A bond. In general, if a bond isn't rated, the company isn't very large or well known and that bond isn't for you. Also you are advised to stick with BBB (or Baa) and higher rated bonds.

Losses on Bonds

It is very easy to lose money on bonds even though they are considered the "safest" of investments. Let's assume you bought a $1,000 U.S. Government bond in 1959 which promised to pay you 4 percent interest each year for 30 years and then would pay you the original $1,000 in 1989. There is little doubt that you will get your interest payment each year and that you will get the $1,000 in 1989, for it is as sure as the U.S. Government and that is about as sure as you can get. If the U.S. Government fails, the chances are you will not need dollars anyway. So you say, "How can I lose?" Well, you can't and won't lose if you never want your money until 1989. But suppose you needed the money in 1974 (to pay a huge medical bill or buy a house or a car, etc.)? You would take this "sure thing" bond to your banker and ask him to sell it and he would—and you might receive $760. The reason is that the buyer of your bond cannot get the $1,000 until 1989 and he can get 6 percent on his money now while you are only getting 4 percent (which was the going rate in 1959). When he offered you $760, he was paying an amount which at 6 percent interest would equal the $1,000 and 4 percent interest which your bond would pay him. He wasn't cheating you or getting a bargain—he just insisted on receiving the going rate of interest. The result is that you (or your widow) lost $240 on a $1,000 investment simply because the rate of interest changed and you needed your money back at the wrong time. Big firms, insurance companies, etc., can wait for the bonds to pay off, but you, as an individual, often cannot do so. You must remember, however, that the interest rate is good, and that the investment is ordinarily secure. The Government does not, of course, insure the value of the bonds of corporations. (If you bought a bond paying high interest rates and the general interest rate fell, the value of the bond might be higher than what you paid for it. However, it seldom seems to work this way, for unless it is a noncallable bond, the company may insist on paying you the full amount ahead of schedule! It's hard to win!)

94

PERSONAL FINANCES FOR MINISTERS

Unhandy Investments

Bonds are "nice" but not very "handy"—the size is often un-wieldy! And when you get your bond what do you do with it? If it is lost or stolen, you've probably lost your money, so you must keep it in a bank vault. If it has coupons on it, you may have to cut the interest coupon off the bond each pay period and send it to the company (or have your bank do it) and then wait for the interest. If you forget to clip the coupon on time, some companies do not remind you and if you are one year late in ask-ing for it, you get what was owed a year ago, but without any interest. To be sure, some companies handle their bond coupon payments better than that. You present your coupon to the teller at your bank, he credits your bank account, and the bank will col-lect from the company. Indeed, some bonds are now issued in registered form, and you receive regular checks for interest. Frankly, bonds are, generally speaking, not for the average min-ister. They are nice to talk about, but let others have the fun of watching over those precious little slips of paper!

If you wish to be more "sophisticated," you can speak of con-vertible bonds and debentures (be sure you know how to pro-nounce that word and put the emphasis on the second syllable!). Bonds are a special field, and in the investment world you have "bond" and "stock" men, and each thinks his area of investment is best. There are plenty of good books on the subject. This is enough on bonds for this "primer" on personal finances.

Common Stocks

We come now to shares of common stocks and there is a con-trast that must be noted between bonds and stocks. If you have a company's bond, you generally do not own a part of the com-pany. You have lent money to those who are running it and they have promised to pay you back with interest. As security, you often have the property of the company, the buildings, machines, plant equipment, etc., so if the company "goes broke," these as-sets may be sold and you, along with the other bondholders, would receive whatever the assets sold for. If you have stock, you are an owner—you have purchased a share of the entire enterprise. As a stockholder you have not lent the company any money and the company need never "pay you back" anything.

The difference between the owners and the lenders is that the former are stockholders, or shareholders, and the latter, the bondholders, are just outside lenders. If the value of the company rises—or if investors generally think the value of the company will rise, the value of each share of stock rises. When we say the value of a share rises, we mean the market value, which is the price that other people would be willing, on a certain day, to pay you for your share.

Just as the market value of a share may rise, it may also fall. Indeed, the daily stock market pages show that every day some stocks rise and some fall. It may be said, in general, and at this writing, that for some years now the value of stocks has been rising. That is in part because the "value" of most companies has risen, and the earnings of those companies have also risen. Another factor influencing the rise in values is that we have experienced considerable inflation in the same years. (When there is inflation, it takes more dollars than was earlier the case to buy the same article or satisfy the same desire. The dollars are worth less than they were, and it takes more of them to buy the same thing.)

Inflation

Therefore, we have two closely related reasons for buying common stocks. One, they rise in real value as the enterprises they represent prosper. Two, the stocks tend to become worth more dollars as inflation decreases the buying power of each dollar. It is customary to lament inflation, and to deplore the deteriorated economic condition of society when inflation is a symptom of that deterioration. Inflation is not necessary and is considered by many persons to be morally wrong. A government can maintain the value of its currency. Even small and relatively underdeveloped countries have been able to do so. Inflation is one way of taking money from those who have it and distributing it to others—it is sometimes more painless than taxation—but the adverse developments resulting from inflation are very serious. (Pardon the brief sermon on economics!) The lamentable fact is that only a few "conservatives" and the pensioners ever rail about inflation. Even the life insurance companies have done relatively little more than "speak strongly" about the subject, perhaps because their agents need to sell more insurance to offset the decreasing value of the dollar. As a hard-boiled, smart investor, you must be conscious of what is happening and act accordingly.

Meanwhile, the problem of the individual investor is not so much to deplore inflation as to equip himself to move with it, and not to be left behind by it, holding perhaps as many dollars as ever, but less valuable dollars. If the dollars are going to be cheap, he must contrive to get more of them so that he can stay even. Investment in common stocks is generally considered to be one way to perform that feat. There have been years when inflation went up and stock values went down—the two are not necessarily related—but historically both have marched together during the past seventy years.

Preferred Stocks

Parenthetically, we have called stocks "common stocks" above. The reason for the modifier is that there are also "preferred stocks." They have a prior claim on the company's earnings, and tend to provide more stable yields than common stocks. For convenience, you may think of preferred stocks as standing between bonds and common stocks, in the matter of safety and yield. A preferred stock generally constitutes a share in the company on which the company promises to pay a certain percent each year. For example, you may buy a 5 percent preferred stock in Company A and when it was issued it probably sold at $100 a share. The company promises to pay you $5 a year for each share of such preferred stock you own, so if the company failed to make a profit last year, it would probably pay the $5 out of its assets even though the company skipped paying any dividends on its common stock. If the company is too hard pressed financially, it may skip paying the $5 on your preferred stock for a year or two, but when it finally starts "operating in the black" (i.e., making money) it will have to pay the $5 a year for the years it skipped to the preferred stock holders first before it pays any dividends to the common stock holders. Preferred stocks are good if you need stable income, but they are not as popular as they were. If interest rates have gone up to 6 percent since you bought the preferred stock paying 5 percent, the price of one share of the preferred will be only $83.33 (because the investor who can get 6 percent on his money elsewhere will pay only that amount on which the company's $5 payment will yield 6 percent, i.e., 6 percent of $83.33 is $5). If interest rates stay high, you may never be able to get your money back in full, i.e., the original $100 you invested. If, on the other hand, interest rates fall below the 5 percent which the preferred was paying, then you will make a profit. It is dangerous to gamble on which way the interest rates will go, since they are subject to government pressures as well as to economic factors. (Anyone with access to sufficient capital who knew that a few months from now the yearly interest rate would be up [or down] by 1 percent could theoretically become a millionaire in a year!)

Foundations

You are advised to invest, somehow, in common stocks. Let us see how institutions do it, and then see whether we can scale down their operations to fit our individual needs. The chairman of the board of one religious foundation recognizes that he is investing money that doesn't belong to him. It is given by others. It is for the use of still others. He knows he must invest in some bonds, as a hedge against a decline in the stock market. He knows he must invest in some stocks, as a hedge against inflation and as a means of making the investment grow. His job—and that of the other trustees—is to have a balanced portfolio, which is financial language for having just the right assortment and mixture of the right kinds of investments. He will never attain that ideal, but he must work toward it.

This board chairman—and he is real, not fictional—urges the purchase of more and more stocks. His colleagues react somewhat in fear: they say a recession would destroy the value of the stocks. This man is convinced that the Government will so act that inflation will continue to erode the value of each dollar. He doesn't like it, and he would like to stop it, but believes he cannot, really, do so. Therefore, he urges his colleagues to take all money in the foundation and divide it equally into investments in stocks and in bonds, 50 percent for bonds, 50 percent for stocks. He then asks that they keep everything that is earned from bonds in one account, so to speak, and everything that is earned from stocks in another. Sell a bond; use that money to buy more bonds. Sell a stock; use that money to buy more stocks. He is convinced that, within a short period, the stock account, which would begin with exactly the same number of dollars as the bond account, would exceed the value of the bond account manyfold.

We recite this situation so that you may see how difficult it would be for you to perform on a small scale the work of those trustees. In a sense, they can afford some mistakes that you can't afford. They can't afford to lose money, but they can afford, as a matter of biding their time, to have a stock severely decline, and then wait for it to rise again. Maybe you can't.

It may seem ludicrous to recommend to the average minister that he maintain a balanced portfolio. It would be nice if the trustees of the above foundation would let you drop your dollars into their investing process, so that all the brains, judgment, and maneuverability of that foundation would be carrying you along. Indeed, you would have ownership of small fragments of each component security of the foundation's balanced portfolio.

Mutual Funds

There is a way you can do somewhat the same thing. You can buy shares in a mutual fund. The officers of the mutual fund operate much like the trustees of the foundation, except that they get paid for it. Some mutual funds seek a large, varied, and balanced portfolio. They may play a little stronger for growth and return than do the foundation people, and they take a few more chances. That is, most mutual funds do as the foundation chairman recommends and invest a larger portion of the assets in stocks rather than bonds.

If you wish to invest in mutual funds, it is important for you to know something about them. There are good funds and poor ones. There are speculative funds and safe funds. There are balanced funds and funds invested only in common stocks. There are growth funds, income funds, real estate funds, chemical funds, and plenty of other types. You must first decide what you want and then select from among the available funds of which there are hundreds.

One adviser says there is a better plan than buying shares in a balanced mutual fund. He suggests that you put part of your funds in a savings bank or savings and loan (since these funds are invested in mortgages, bonds, etc.) and the other part in a common stock mutual fund. The portion in the savings account would be readily available to you without loss, and without the need for liquidating your mutual fund shares and yet you would be creating your own "balanced" fund.

Why Common Stocks

If you are participating in Social Security, you have purchased a considerable amount of insurance and have a fairly good hedge against inflation (if there is inflation in the future, an increase in Social Security benefits will almost certainly be voted). If you are also a member of your church pension plan, you have probably provided adequately for your retirement years and you can expect your church to be reasonably conservative with its money. If you have some life insurance, a modest checking account, and a savings account of at least fourth months' salary, and if you still have some money to invest, you are in a position to assume a little more risk in the investment of your money. We believe that you could properly invest all of this extra money in mutual funds that invest wholly in common stocks. While you are young, you may invest more in lower yielding growth stocks, for you do not need interest income on which you pay income tax—you want a large capital fund when you are older. If you are a few years from retirement or actually in retirement, you want fairly regular and good income and you do not want to wait for growth to materialize—you probably won't live that long. For the average minister, who is not too analytical about his financial needs, a mutual fund that is balanced between growth and income would be generally satisfactory.

Selection of a Mutual Fund

When you pick a mutual fund, pick one whose directors are known and have standing and a fund large enough so that it cannot easily be manipulated. Remember that when you give your money to the fund, the directors have the right to invest the money in almost any way they wish. If there is a sudden change in economic conditions, these men will be under great pressures and they just might be tempted to sell General Motors and invest in Podunk Electronics (to save the company whose president is somebody's father-in-law). Remember, these managers are using your money, not theirs, and they must be men who accept responsibility and can maintain their composure in adversity, which some of the more brilliant younger men would not do. Remember, too, that Fund A may have had a brilliant record over the past five years by a lucky guess or two and look much better than Fund B, but in the next ten years Fund B may profit from their sound, long-range planning while Fund A may this time guess wrong. (It is very difficult to compare records between funds, but you should review the available records anyway, for they will eliminate a goodly number from further consideration.)

Do not invest in mutual funds unless you expect to leave the money in the fund for at least five years, preferably ten. Most funds have a "loading" charge to cover the sales and distribution of the shares, which varies between funds and is published information (just ask for the pamphlets each fund issues as a "prospectus"). This charge in the past has been 5 percent to 10 percent—averaging about 8 percent. It is a single charge that is made only once. If the fund is properly managed and does an intelligent job for you, this will be worth much more than 8 percent—not very large if it is to cover a period of ten years or more, possibly forty years. To look up basic facts about these funds, ask your broker (or banker) to let you see a copy of Wiesenberger's analysis of mutual funds and study it. Some daily papers carry a listing of mutual funds—near the stock market quotations—or you can obtain any day's copy of *The Wall Street Journal* and the alphabetical listing would look like this:

Mutual Funds

	Bid	Asked	Bid Chg		Bid	Asked	Bid Chg
Keystone Custodian Funds:							
Invst B 1 ...	21.09	22.01	+ .02	Lifelns Inv	5.79	6.33	— .04
MedG B 2 ...	22.21	24.24	— .03	Lifelns Stk	4.14	4.53	— .02
Disct B 4 ...	9.65	10.53	......				
Incm K 1 ...	8.80	9.61	— .03	Loomis Sayles Funds (v):			
Grth K 2 ...	6.13	6.70	— .01	Canadn	31.94	31.94	— .06
HihGr S 1 ..	20.85	22.72	—1.12	Cap Dev	11.27	11.27	— .03
Incm S 2 ...	10.54	11.50	— .02	Mutual	14.64	14.64	......
Grwth S 3 ..	9.20	10.04	+ .01	Manhattn	9.84	10.76	— .03
LowP S 4 ...	6.45	7.04	— .02	Mass Fund	11.42	12.48	+ .02
Keystn Intl	14.33	15.50	— .01	Mass Grth	11.16	12.20	— .01
Knickr Fd	7.06	7.73	— .02	Mass In Tr	15.14	16.55	......
Knickr Gth	10.65	11.66	+ .03	Mates Inv	5.83	5.83	+ .03
Lex Inc Tr	9.73	10.63	......	McDonll	10.98	12.03	— .02
Lex Resch	14.27	15.60	— .03	Mid Amer	6.77	7.40	— .04
Liberty Fd	7.86	8.04	— .01	Moody Cap	15.15	16.56	— .05

The difference between Bid and Asked is the "loading" or commission you pay on the purchase of the shares. For example, if you were to buy MIT (listed above as Mass In Tr, which stands for Massachusetts Investors Trust) shares on the day the above report was made, you would pay $16.55 for each share, but it would be worth $15.14, so that is all you would get for it if you sold it the same day. (Remember that if you bought the stocks represented in the portfolio yourself, you would have to pay a commission to buy them and an equal commission were you to sell them. So your "loading" is not all lost. It covers both the buying and selling costs.)

There are "no load" funds and the records of these funds has generally been almost as good as the "load" funds. These funds charge no initial sales commission and the fund managers get paid from the management fees they collect from the operation of the fund itself. These fees generally are the same in both load and no-load funds. No broker or banker is interested in selling you a no-load fund. So if you want to invest in such funds, you have to take the initiative yourself, and virtually insist that they take your money. They will, but the service is normally inferior and no one bothers to tell you that you are making a good investment.

Actually, the purchase of a no-load fund is essentially a purchase from the company, direct and without participation by local brokers or bankers. You can look in *The Wall Street Journal* or the big-city dailies for advertisements or information about such funds.

Ministers will have no difficulty in getting good advice from brokers on mutual funds that pay a commission, but they will find few persons willing and competent to recommend a no-load fund. One of the older, larger, and well-managed mutual funds invested wholly in common stocks (ownership of which constitutes owning a "slice of American industry") is the Massachusetts Investment Trust Fund. This fund's objective is to provide a combination of reasonable income with reasonable capital appreciation. It would be of particular interest to the older and fairly conservative investor. They also manage the Massachusetts Investors Growth Stock Fund, which seeks capital appreciation rather than income. This fund's objective would appeal to the young and more optimistic investor. For the no-load growth-type funds, T. Rowe

Price, Loomis Sayles, and Scudder Stevens & Clark are responsible firms with good managements. The T. Rowe Price funds have been almost spectacularly effective in recent years. There are hundreds of such funds and many have been much more "successful" in the past ten years than those mentioned, but the next ten years could yield a different result.

Accounting Procedures

One of the joys of dealing with a mutual fund is that it takes all your money and you are never bothered with little dribs and drabs of dividend checks and voting on directors of companies about whom you have never heard. A good mutual fund will accept anything—anytime—perhaps $200 initially, $29.57 ten days later, nothing for six months, etc. It reports that you bought 6.234 shares with that last check you sent in and now have 18.743 shares total. The mutual fund usually pays a dividend (not to be confused with the dividends it receives from its investments of your money). At the end of the calendar year it tells you how much of your dividends are current income and how much capital gains, for income tax purposes. Indeed, the whole thing is summarized for you as to taxes. During the year, the fund has reinvested the dividends so that money is making money for you. (This process and procedure is quite different from buying and selling specific common stock shares, which can get complicated.)

One word of caution: Do not ever sign an agreement under which you are obligated to invest regularly certain sums each month in a mutual or other type of fund. There is no need to do so—just send your money in regularly and you will get equal consideration. In some of these contracts—known as "front end loading"—the salesman collects commission on all the future payments you have promised to pay, and if for some reason (such as death or disability) you have to stop, you can lose a considerable sum of money.

Not Recommended

In general, we do not recommend that ministers and their families venture directly into the stock market to buy individual stocks. We assume that the unusual minister who is keenly equipped to deal successfully with the stock market is not reading these pages in any case. For the others, we believe that such investments may be too time-consuming and too worrisome—especially if the wife reads the papers every day and reminds her husband of what he "lost." (She will generally say little about the advances.) Many persons are not psychologically able to remain objective about their own money, and they become obsessed with the ups and downs of the market in a particular stock. Such persons should stay away from the direct ownership of stocks.

Stock Purchases

If you insist on purchasing some stocks, the following is included as a primer and basic guideline.

It is very simple and easy to invest in stocks, but you should understand the "other man's problems." Let us assume that you decide to buy the stock of Company A and have $500 to invest. If you are in a city, you will go to a brokerage office, walk in, and tell the broker what you want! (The next transaction you might handle over the telephone or by letter, but not the first one.) If you are in a small town, you will have to handle it through a bank. The person who handles it probably won't question you as to why you are buying that particular stock—he will just proceed! If you ask him, he will give you his opinion about the stock—if it is well known—but he will probably hedge and suggest that you study the facts yourself. (All banks and brokers have big looseleaf books that contain information about almost every company, its finances, the history of the value of the stock for at least the past ten years, its dividend records, etc. It is all freely available and there is no charge to look at it in their offices.) A good brokerage office can and will help you in many ways, and if they know you are inexperienced and open to suggestion, they will give you good, safe advice. However, if a customer wants to buy speculative stock in Company X, they will keep discreetly silent. (The top men in large offices are generally well informed on investments, but they are not omniscient. Remember that if brokers really knew what was going to happen, they would all be millionaires and probably wouldn't bother coming into the office every day to work with customers who have only $500 to invest!)

You will, of course, be buying stock on the New York or American Stock Exchange. (There are other stocks, listed on other stock exchanges, or over-the-counter [OTC listings], but they are *not* for you. You can also buy Japanese, Mexican, German, Swiss, and other stocks, but as a neophyte, these are *not* for you.) When you express interest in Company A, the broker will probably pick up the local paper or *The Wall Street Journal* and look at the listings which will give him an idea of yesterday's prices. You probably would have already done it in the column that looks like this:

New York Stock Exchange Transactions

| —1967-68— | | | | Sales in | | | | | Net |
High	Low		Div.	100s	Open	High	Low	Last	chg.
17⅞	13	Abacus	.70f	5	16½	16½	16½	16½	— ⅛
53⅞	41	Abbott Lab	1	173	44¼	44¾	44	44⅜	— ⅜
34⅞	27⅞	Abex Cp	1.60	14	30¼	30¾	30¼	30⅝	+ ½
58¼	38⅛	ACF Ind	2.20	718	46	46¼	45	45⅛	— ⅝
46¾	32	Acme Mkt	2b	12	38¼	38½	38	38¼	+ ¼
34	27	AdamE	2.35e	4	32	32	32	32	+ ¼
87¼	14½	AdMills	.40a	82	58⅝	59⅛	55	56¼	—2¼
80½	46⅞	Address	1.40	92	77	77⅜	75⅜	76½	+ ½
38	18⅛	Admiral		100	19½	19½	19	19⅛	.....
69⅛	35	Aeroquip	1b	16	59⅞	62	59⅞	62	+2⅛
46¼	31⅝	Air Prod	20b	34	36½	37	36½	36¾	+ ¼
44⅞	32⅛	Air Redtn	1.50	43	36¾	36⅞	36½	36½	.....

From this, he knows that the number of shares traded yesterday in Abbott Laboratories (a pharmaceutical drug company) was 17,300 and somebody paid as much as 44¾ per share while others bought the same shares for as little as 44, and the last purchase for the day was at 44⅜. He also sees that the stock was up to 53⅞ per share and down to 41 per share during the last year. (He can look up its high and low for earlier years in his reference book.) The broker then can generally get a direct quotation over the wires (or by telephone) indicating what it is at that minute. In most large offices this takes about fifteen seconds. He generally checks the quotation, for it might have gone up or down several points in the last several hours, on the basis of some news that others may have heard and that is not generally known yet. He then asks what you will be willing to pay for it.

Your answer should probably be "at the market." You may be lucky and get it at the "low" for the day, or you may be unlucky that your order arrived in New York City at 11:33 A.M. and the stock was trading at its highest for the day! The fact is that you haven't analyzed the stock carefully enough (and nobody could) to know whether it is worth 44¼ or 44¾ per share. Be brave and hope for the best. (You could say that you would not pay more than 44½ for it, but this complicates matters a little. The shares are traded in 100 unit blocks and someone has to combine your small purchase with others to make the offer, etc. Therefore, it is possible that you will not be able to buy it at that price. However, if you insist, the broker will follow your instructions.)

Now, having made the request, you'd think you could write out a check and wait for the stock certificates. Not so. The broker doesn't know what the cost will be and his commission is based, in part, on the exact price of the stock. If you establish an account with him, he will bill you for the right amount when he knows what it will be (usually within hours). If no account is established, you'll have to give him an approximate amount and it will need to be adjusted later. His charge for one transaction involving the purchase of 10 shares of stock worth $50 will be about $10.50. It is a standard charge, which is a percentage of the total transaction, plus a small fixed charge (it gets much smaller if you buy in large amounts), and since all brokers charge exactly the same amount, there is no point in shopping around.

Since the price of a stock is variable and you always get it in 1/8th point jumps (i.e., the price is 50, or 50⅜ or 50¼ [2/8th] or 50⅝—but never $50.17), it just isn't possible to invest $500 exactly. You can buy 2, or 11, or 63 shares—any number. But the chances are that, with the commission, it will never come out $500 exactly. It is generally not feasible to buy a fraction of one share of stock.

The MIP Procedure

There is a plan that has been worked out by the stock exchange which the brokers refer to as the MIP (Monthly Investment Plan) which allows you to put a specified sum each month into a program and the money is invested in the stocks of your choice. This is helpful though a little costly. If you invest less than $100 a month, the purchasing commission is about 6 percent, and when you sell, there will be another commission payable and you may not be getting as good investment counsel as you may have with a well-selected mutual fund. The plan is good, however, and it does allow you to skip a month or discontinue the plan at any time.

Some Housekeeping Problems

Buying stock offers other problems, because a week or two after purchase you get a certificate. This is a valuable piece of paper and you must take care of it, for if you lose it, you probably won't ever get any of the money back. If the certificate falls into the hands of an unscrupulous person, he will have arranged to sell the stock. If the certificate is burned, the company may not have it registered except by number and if you don't have the number, the company may not be able to find you in its records, etc. (Some investors have the broker keep the stock for them, and this is O.K. if it is a good brokerage office and if he doesn't go out of business.) Then someday you'll get a check for a few dollars as dividends paid on those few shares, which isn't enough to buy another share, so after carrying the check around a few days you just cash it and spend it. These are a few of the problems of owning just a little stock. This is why it is usually best for a minister to buy shares in a mutual fund, where they take it all, invest it all, keep it invested, and you just get a report once or twice a year on the results (with enough information to complete your income tax returns easily). This latter system of investing is much simpler and is generally recommended for ministers.

Nine Basic Rules

The following advice has stood the test of time. You are advised to take all of it. It may sound very simple, but it is very important for the small investor who insists on making his own stock investments.

1. Own only stocks of leading companies in sound and essential industries.

2. Own only stocks that are listed on a registered securities exchange or that conform to exchange requirements.

3. Own only stocks that can boast an earnings or dividend record—or both—unbroken for at least ten years.

4. Own a few low-yield stocks as a means of building up capital and future income. (The virtue of the apparently negative term "low yield" is that a company that plows back into its op-

erations a considerable share of its earnings, instead of paying the earnings out to you as dividends, is increasing its net worth. Since you own a part of the company, your share is getting more and more valuable toward the day when you convert it to spendable cash—perhaps in retirement.)

5. Diversify your holdings in at least five different industries (utilities, oils, chemicals, drugs, manufacturing, office equipment, mining, etc.).

6. Own stocks in fairly equal amounts in at least ten companies.

7. Once a year sell at least one stock, choosing the weakest on the list with no consideration whatever for its original cost. Replace it with a more attractive stock.

8. Do not be disturbed by losses on individual risks, but keep an eye out for gain or loss on the aggregate.

9. Subscribe to one high-grade financial publication and read it regularly and thoroughly.

An Image Problem

To do a good job you will need to work at it. As a minister, your lay constituency will look askance if you show too much interest in the stock market. There will be talk about your readership of a financial publication and it is never wise to study the stock listings in the newspaper in public. Such small matters do often affect a minister's influence on the community and sometimes his salary. It is for these reasons that most ministers should not invest directly in particular stocks. It does take a surprisingly large amount of time to do it well. Our advice is to let the managers of a carefully selected mutual fund do it for you. After you have accumulated $50,000 plus in such investments, then maybe you might try it yourself on your additional accumulations.

Real Estate

There is much to be said for real estate as an investment, but little to be said for it in the case of ministers. We put aside first the possibility of purchasing a share in a real estate syndicate, which may be putting up large apartment houses. There is reason to believe that the potential returns in such ventures have been exaggerated. Investment in operations where you have no personal involvement is done better in the securities market, preferably by way of mutual funds.

The more pressing question for ministers is the ownership of a piece of real estate personally known to the owner: for example, his own residence. Over 75 percent of the readers of these pages will have the use of manses or parsonages owned by their congregations. For such a minister, the ownership of a residence during his career is not a live question. For the others, it is possible to buy a house from a housing allowance provided by the congregation. In general, we advise you not to use a housing allowance to buy a residence. Use it to rent the facilities you need.

The ownership of a house in your present community could be a factor keeping you from accepting a call to another community. Moreover, owning your own house so you will have a place to live in retirement is good for many people but not good for ministers. If you own a house where you serve, that will be the house you live in when you retire. Putting two and two together, we now have you retired and living in the midst of your former people, and therefore in a position to do mischief for your successor: innocent mischief, but a trial even among saints. Even if you have a halo around your head, your wife may not have—and your children may have their halos slip in trying to "defend the old man." You should leave the community of your last pastorate as surely as you left all the communities before. You may think you would be an exception to this general rule, but the chances are that the man who thinks he is an exception will prove to be the very one who is not.

To own a house in one community and keep it when you move elsewhere puts you in the business of holding real estate purely as an investment. That can be very difficult as well as a poor investment. For proof, see the New Testament stories of unfaithful stewards who did not take care of the land and property of the true owner, because they were hirelings. You can have problems with both the reckless tenant and the less than diligent real estate manager. Own only real estate in an area where you are living and where you can attend to it personally. Otherwise, you are taking a gamble as everyone else who has tried it finds out.

Most ministers are not hard-boiled enough to make good land-lords. Of course, if your house is a shambles and your wife is a very poor housekeeper, you could try renting for a while! Our basic advice is: Do not invest in real estate in a community in which you are a pastor to a congregation.

A Vacation Home

There is something in human nature that makes a person want to call a piece of ground his own. If you have that good instinct and also are committed to the mountains as a way of vacationing, you may find it good to fulfill your real estate instinct by buying a cabin or cottage. Some ministers have cleansed their spirits of their vocational trials by building—building onto—their vacation retreats. Your equity in it could well be the source of funds for housing in your retirement. Be sure, however, that such a retreat, if it involves much money, can be protected from fire, flood, and termites and that it can be insured at less than prohibitive rates. We do not urge upon you the purchase of vacation housing, but we should mention its possibilities. One word of caution: Do not winterize it and plan to live in it in retirement. We can assure you that it will not be in the right location for a retirement residence.

Another word of caution: Do not buy a lot by mail. See any piece of land before you buy it. The desert in Arizona can indeed blossom like a rose in many places, but the water pipes may not yet—or ever—be laid to your lot. The sandy location in Florida that looks so good in pictures may be covered with water a portion of the year and it's no fun shopping in a rowboat or having your house sink slowly.

Summary

In summary, then, investing is putting your resources to work where they will at least earn interest for you and preferably also grow in value. The ideal investment would be highly productive of earnings, would grow mightily in value, and would be absolutely secure. Success in investing is finding that middle ground where all three considerations are served as much as possible.

Chapter 9

RETIREMENT

These few paragraphs on retirement from the active ministry come last. They do so, of course, because retirement comes last in the financial stages of our lives. Moreover, retirement is a kind of final grade given for your study and practice of the management of your money. If you have spent well, borrowed wisely, saved carefully, invested prudently, and insured sensibly, you should be able to retire well—at least financially. It is the ultimate proof of the rightness of your financial program.

It is a pity that geriatric advice of all kinds, including financial advice, tends to be handed out by people too young to have retired. This author can only guess, from the lower side of sixty-five years, that retirement has problems that the young probably cannot fully comprehend.

One fact with which to begin is to note that people are getting healthier and living longer. That should mean that they have more productive years to give than their forebears, and they should be allowed to work longer, i.e., to make more of a contribution to society. There are other contributions that a person can make to society—other than work—and it is in this area that much needs to be done. Ministers will need to lead the way. It can be revolutionary in a constructive sense, but such changes must come. Perhaps volunteer service under a better name by the elderly can be the makings of a new civilization—both more Christian and more progressive.

A "Free" Man

Your parishioners will be watching hopefully for a guideline. They will watch to see what you do—their minister who lived among them but for others, who served where he was "called" (not where he wanted to be), who served on modest salaries, who espoused unpopular causes, who encouraged them when they were despondent, etc. At last, in retirement, you are free of all responsibility, you can live anywhere in the world, you receive a reasonably adequate income, you can do anything you want to do— yes, you will be a totally free man! What will you do? This perhaps will be your golden opportunity to show the way to a better life.

Eleven Items of Advice

Let us see whether there is generalized advice for persons embarking on retirement. Let us see whether that advice is sensible enough to be accepted.

1. You should realize that you will be restricted in your "borrowing" after you retire. Lenders will not look upon you as a good risk. When they lent you money when you were younger, they were in part betting on your longevity and on your earning an income. Now at retirement, you haven't very much of either going for you. At seventy, you won't be able to get a thirty-year mortgage on the house you wish to buy. (The lender doesn't expect you to live to be one hundred—and he doesn't want your house back.) If you get sick on your reduced income, you may not be able to pay the regular monthly payment—and he doesn't want the community to think of him as a Scrooge, so he really can't get you out of the house while you are sick! What could he do really? Actually, nothing. He knows this and will stay out of trouble by not lending the money. It isn't that he doesn't trust you. It's the other factors!

2. Your retirement plan should take into account the fact that you and your wife will probably not die at the same time. That means there will be a survivor. If the survivor is your wife, be sure adequate provision is made for her when she will be living alone.

3. Leave the community in which you have concluded your ministry. It is always possible that you are an unflawed and unfaulted saint who could not possibly be the focus of any trouble for the new pastor. If by chance you are, it is possible that your wife may not be! And, if miraculously both of you are saints, maybe one of your children who lives in the area is not as perfect

as the parents. Leave town! If this just isn't possible, leave town for a year or two and then come back, even if it costs you a little money, for it will be the best contribution you could make to the church and to the community! If you must return, good advice is to unite with another area congregation, not with the one last served!

4. Since you will be leaving the town in which you last served, plan for it a few years ahead. Know where you are going to go, and what it is going to cost to live there. Rent a year before you buy, unless you have lived before in the place to which you are going. Be sure you can pass the examination for a new driver's license if you will be living in a different state!

5. Announce your intended retirement at a decent interval beforehand—at least six months. Frankly, it gives people a chance to see you fondly as one who will, at a known time, be gone! It lets them think about the financial assistance you may need in retirement. It gives some officer a chance to wonder aloud whether the congregation shouldn't pay your moving bill. It preoccupies them with things that might be done for a man who will soon be beyond the reach of their kindnesses, rather than with irritants that might otherwise be on their minds—especially if they have wondered whether you would ever retire!

6. Do not commit yourself irrevocably to any retirement home or village without exploring it thoroughly. Visit the place. Visit with the people already living there. Know for sure what it costs and anticipate increased costs. Be especially careful of any arrangement that requires you to sign over all that you have and all that you have hope of getting. Remember: Managements change, admission rules and requirements can change, taxes may go up and some places do go bankrupt, and your health or your wife's may require a change in climate.

7. Know—and this you could really know a good many years before you retire—how much you will have to live on. At age fifty-five, inquire in writing what pension benefits you may expect from your church pension plan and also from Social Security. If you have served more than one denomination, obtain the information about paid-up or fully vested pension credits held by other groups. If your wife has worked, she may have some pension

credits too.   Do not guess or estimate it yourself.   Get it in writing from an authoritative source. Also, determine what your pension would be if your wife dies and what it would be if you die. Sometimes, the pension plan allows options that can adjust the income more equitably. As a rough rule of thumb, your assured pension income should be about 60 percent to 75 percent of your final salary if that salary is $6,000 or less and about 40 percent if that final salary is $20,000 or higher. Remember that you can live comfortably on less income after retirement without reducing your standard of living and that your needs and desires will probably decrease an average of perhaps 2 percent to 3 percent a year after retirement. Know what is available in church-operated homes, in special housing for the retired, and in nursing homes in the area of your planned retirement, but do not be overly concerned about them. It is unlikely that you or your wife will ever be in one of them, but you owe it to yourself to know about them. (Visit them when you are sixty—when it may be ten to twenty years before you could be interested and when you can still be "objective." You will be surprised how nice some of them are.)   In planning your retirement, consider using a good portion of the capital and savings you have accumulated. Do not try to save it for your children. Use it to visit them or to have them visit you.

8.   Stop paying premiums on almost all of your life insurance policies.   Keep one for a "clean up" fund, if you wish, but put it on a paid-up basis.   You should insure for a purpose and when the purpose ends or disappears, you should not continue to carry the insurance.   Consider the money you have in your insurance policies as investments.   Use the cash values as an investment (put in a savings account, etc.) or buy an annuity which may pay you 7%–10% interest depending upon your age, if you wish, but don't keep paying on your ordinary life policy just because you have done so for forty years.

9.   Enroll in Medicare as soon as possible.   You can do so at age sixty-five even though you are active—and your wife can do so independently of you whenever she attains age sixty-five.   This plan, to which you will need to make a monthly contribution for medical care, provides both hospital and medical costs with very small deductibles.   It provides the basic health coverage everyone

needs. Buy additional health insurance if it will give you some psychological comfort—but most persons will find it better to self-insure. Most older persons have a tendency to overinsure!

10. Don't work too hard in retirement but work some. It will be a very wise retired man who knows how much "employment" to accept in retirement. It is wise to retire in an area where there will be opportunities to serve, but then be wise enough to "turn down" some requests! If you do work for money, make sure it's worth it: Social Security and pension plans tend to stop paying at certain levels of earned income, so know what the limits are before you make final arrangements.

11. Retire before you have to and move to your new home while you and your wife are healthy enough to make new friends. It isn't easy to make friends if you arrive in a new community on a stretcher. You can always find meaningful work to do wherever you are, so go where you want to retire and begin your new life. This time perhaps you'd better go where your wife will be happy, for surely you can make the adjustment more easily. If she isn't happy, you won't be for long!

A Closing Word

And now, in closing, we hope we have not either overwhelmed you with details or confused you with generalizations. We hope, too, that you will give these suggestions a good, honest "try." We know that we have not fully kept our Foreword pledge not to preach at you, but we have tried. If at times we have seemed guilty of self-ascribed omniscience, please forgive us. We know we don't know it all. Our only claim is that we have tried to read the right books, to consult the right authorities, and to put the right construction on our own experiences with financial matters. We hope we have not been so rigorous or demanding that we have left you behind, even as you have sometimes known that you have, in a sermon, left a whole congregation behind. We hope that you will take that portion of our counsel which seems possible and reasonable. Even when you are doing what we have suggested that you not do, please be sure to know what you are doing and why you are doing it. You could be right! And we hope so.

Fortune is a two-sided word. Sometimes we use it to describe our financial situation as when young men used to set out to seek their fortunes, or as when brave men pledged "our lives, our fortunes, and our sacred honor." At other times, we are just talking about luck, and we can wish someone good fortune in somewhat the same way as we wish him good luck. We want things to happen according to your plan and to turn out well for you, especially those events and dimensions of life over which you have little or no control. Good fortune is to have good health. Good fortune is to have no accidents, no fires, no heartbreaks.

In both senses of the word, we wish you good fortune. We hope you will have plenty of money to do the good things you want to do. We hope also that things will go well for you.

Appendix

MONEY MANAGEMENT RECORDS

Each family will have its own way of keeping its records. The following pages give some examples of what could and should be kept basically. One should be reminded that one person in the family could have all these facts available to him or her, but if that person suddenly becomes ill or dies, the remaining family members often are at a loss to know where to find the facts.

The record charts are as follows:

1. Year-End Review for Calendar Year
2. Year-End Inventory—Family Net Worth
3. Family Document Finder
4. Family Life Insurance Record
5. Health, Property, Car, Insurance Record
6. Savings and Checking Accounts
7. Investment Record
8. Family Spending Record for Month of _____, 19____ (a daily listing of expenditures)

Chart 1.   YEAR-END REVIEW FOR CALENDAR YEAR _____

Income for the 12 months, including investment
  income . . . . $_____

      Spent on living a total of . . $_____

      Paid in federal and state in-
      come taxes (and city wage
      taxes) . . . . $_____

      Added to savings and in-
      vestments, and/or repaid
      on general debts . . . . . . $_____

           TOTAL . . . . $_____

TOTAL OF 12 MONTHS' SPENDING
(Excludes Savings and Taxes)

	Total Actually Spent for Year	Compared with Spending Plan for Year
Food	_____	_____
Housing	_____	_____
Clothing	_____	_____
Medical care	_____	_____
Transportation	_____	_____
Advancement	_____	_____
Gifts	_____	_____
Personal care	_____	_____
Entertainment	_____	_____
Allowances, misc. . .	_____	_____
Life insurance	_____	_____
Totals	$_____	$_____

Chart 2.   YEAR-END INVENTORY
Family Net Worth at end of Calendar Year ————

Cash and Securities

Cash on hand and in banks and
savings accounts .... $————

Current insurance cash-surrender
value (as shown on policies) .. $————

Cash value in retirement and
other funds (other than Social
Security and church pension
plan) .... $————

Stocks, mutual fund shares (market value) .... $————

Other .... $————

Property

Equity in house and other real
estate (estimated market value
less mortgage balance) ..... $————

Equity in car (previous year's
value less 29% for past year's
depreciation) .... $————

Other valuable marketable pos-
sessions, as boat, trailer, etc.
(at estimated market value)
(exclude furniture and books) $————

Total Assets $————

Less Debt Balance (Excluding Mortgage)

(Creditor)———————— $————
(Creditor)———————— $————
(Creditor)———————— $————
(Creditor)———————— $————
(Creditor)———————— $————

Total Debts $————

NET WORTH $————
(Assets less Debts)

Chart 3.   FAMILY DOCUMENT FINDER

Our safe-deposit box is located at —————————————————

The key is at ————— Box No. ————— Key No. —————

	Safe-deposit box	Family filing cabinet	Other location (specify)
Wills			
Husband's	☐	☐	—————
Executor —————			
Wife's	☐	☐	—————
Executor —————			
Property deeds, title insurance policy	☐	☐	—————
Mortgage contract	☐	☐	—————
Mortgage payment or rent receipts	☐	☐	—————
Property tax receipts	☐	☐	—————
Insurance policies:			
Life	☐	☐	—————
Accident and health	☐	☐	—————
Property	☐	☐	—————
Automobile	☐	☐	—————
Marriage certificate	☐	☐	—————
Birth certificates	☐	☐	—————
Service discharge	☐	☐	—————
Stock, mutual fund certificates	☐	☐	—————
U.S. savings bonds	☐	☐	—————

	Safe-deposit box	Family filing cabinet	Other location (specify)
Savings account books	☐	☐	_____
Canceled checks, bank statements	☐	☐	_____
Pension plan or annuity contract	☐	☐	_____
Guarantee certificates on car, appliances, other purchases ...	☐	☐	_____
Bills of sale (car, other property)	☐	☐	_____
Installment contracts	☐	☐	_____
Important receipts, paid notes	☐	☐	_____
_____	☐	☐	_____
_____	☐	☐	_____
_____	☐	☐	_____
_____	☐	☐	_____
_____	☐	☐	_____
Property improvement bills ...	☐	☐	_____
Previous income tax returns ..	☐	☐	_____
Records of medical treatment, disability claims	☐	☐	_____
School records—diplomas	☐	☐	_____
Naturalization papers	☐	☐	_____
Other _____	☐	☐	_____
_____	☐	☐	_____
_____	☐	☐	_____
_____	☐	☐	_____

Chart 4. FAMILY

DUE DATES		PREMIUM	COMPANY	PERSON INSURED	POLICY NO.

Chart 5. HEALTH, PROPERTY,

DUE DATES		PREMIUM	COMPANY	POLICY OR PLAN NO.

Chart 6. SAVINGS

IN NAME OF	FINANCIAL INSTITUTION	AMOUNTS FOR			
		EDUCATION	RESERVE	VACATION	OTHER

LIFE INSURANCE RECORD

AMOUNT	BENEFICIARY	AGENT	CURRENT CASH VALUE 19____	19____	19____	19____	19____

CAR, INSURANCE RECORD

AGENT	TYPE OF BENEFITS

AND CHECKING ACCOUNTS

INTEREST RECEIVED 19____	19____	19____	19____	19____	YEAR-END BALANCE 19____	19____	19____	19____	19____

Chart 7. INVESTMENT

STOCKS, BONDS, FUND SHARES	NUMBER BOUGHT	DATE BOUGHT	PURCHASE PRICE SHARE	TOTAL

RECORD

DIVIDENDS (cash, stock)										DATE SOLD	SALE PRICE SHARE	SALE PRICE TOTAL	GAIN OR LOSS
19___		19___		19___		19___		19___					

Chart 8. FAMILY SPENDING RECORD FOR MONTH OF _____, 19___

Date	FOOD		HOUSING			CLOTHING		MEDICAL CARE		TRANSPORTATION		
	At Home	Outside	Rent or Mortgage, Prop. Tax	Utilities, Cleaning Supplies	Insurance, Furnishings, Repairs	Purchases	Cleaning, Repairs	Health Insurance	Doctors, Medicines	Car Payment, Gas, Oil	Repairs, Insurance	Other Fares
1												
2												
3												
4												
5												
28												
29												
30												
31												
TOTALS												
Spending Plan	$		$			$		$		$		

Notes on Unusual Expense Entries: